MINNESOTA'S LOST GOLF COURSES

PART II

JOE BISSEN

FIVE STAR PUBLISHING
South St. Paul, Minnesota

More! Gone. Minnesota's Lost Golf Courses, Part Two

© 2020 Joe Bissen

Published by:
Five Star Publishing
South St. Paul, MN

www.ForeGoneGolf.com

All rights reserved. No part of this book may be reproduced or transmitted in any form or by any means, electronic or mechanical, including photocopying, recording, or by any information storage and retrieval system, without permission in writing from the publisher, except for the inclusion of brief quotations in a review.

COVER: From a peak atop Great Bluffs State Park midway between Winona and La Crosse, Wis., the Mississippi River and land near the abandoned Riverdale Golf Course (1931-40) can be seen. The old golf course site isn't visible from this bluff, but if you took a couple of wrong steps off the platform, you could tumble down toward the old nine-holer, which lay 500 feet below and about a half-mile northeast.

Photos on pages vi and 155 courtesy of Peter Wong.

Cover and interior design, Tamara Dever, TLC Book Design,
www.TLCBookDesign.com

Stock images:

Dreamstime.com; Golfer in circle: © Daveh900 | Dreamstime.com; Nail heads: © Nuttapong | Dreamstime.com; Minnesota counties map: © Deskcube | Baseball, © Depositphotos.com/AlphaBaby | Wooden direction sign, © Depositphotos.com/denisismagilov

ISBN: 978-0-9911748-1-2

To Florence Bissen,
who enjoyed golf but more importantly
helped instill in her son a sense of curiosity
and an appreciation of people and places.

*"The more you play it,
the less you know about it."*

PATTY BERG

ACKNOWLEDGEMENTS

To Tami Dever, co-owner and founder of TLC Book Design of Austin, Texas, whose inimitable artistic touch has twice now made my work more presentable.

To Peter Wong, whose brilliant photography has graced these pages a second time.

To Warren Ryan, Joe Oberle and everyone with the Minnesota Golf Association.

To the Minnesota Historical Society — I hope I haven't worn out too many of your microfilm viewers — and to scores of employees and volunteers at historical societies across the state, and the state immediately east. Special thanks to Wendy Davis of the Mille Lacs County Historical Society and Judy Scholin of the Pine City Area History Association.

To the University of Minnesota, its John Borchert Map Library and its MHAPO historic aerial photo database. Nothing cooler than poking around and finding, *voila!* proof of greens and fairways that were there 85 or 90 years ago.

To those who have consistently supported these crazy chases of mine, among them Rick Shefchik, Chuck Lennon, Fred Taylor, Dan Goodenough, Dee Forsberg McCullach, Randy LaFoy and Tad Reeve.

To family, which has consistently endured the crazy chases: Andy, Nick, Katie and Susie.

TABLE OF CONTENTS

1
INTRODUCTION

3
CHAPTER 1
THE LEFTY IS ALL RIGHT

5
CHAPTER 2
BIG HITTER, SO TO SPEAK
*McAllen Golf Course,
Pokegama Township*

11
CHAPTER 3
TOM AND TOM AGAIN
Hinckley Golf Course, Hinckley

17
CHAPTER 4
THREE COURSES, TWO GOLFERS,
ONE GOOD SPORT
Luverne Golf Club, Luverne

23
CHAPTER 5
TOUGH TIMES

29
CHAPTER 6
OUI, JE CROIS JE L'AVOIR TROUVÉ
*Course: Red Lake Falls Golf Club,
Red Lake Falls*

35
CHAPTER 7
COMFORT ZONE
Minnetonka Country Club, Shorewood

45
CHAPTER 8
PIONEERING AND VANISHING ACT
Silver Creek Golf Club, Rochester

51
CHAPTER 9
COMMON THREADS

55
CHAPTER 10
BACK HOME ON THE FARM
Rush City Country Club, Rush City

61
CHAPTER 11
MINNEAPOLIS MYSTERY
Camden Park Golf Club, Minneapolis

67
CHAPTER 12
FUN AND GAMES
Castle Greens Country Club, Oakdale

73
CHAPTER 13
PICTURE THIS
Twin Valley Golf Club, Twin Valley

77
CHAPTER 14
FAMED FLIGHT, NOT-SO-FAMED
GOLF COURSE
Madelia Golf Club, Madelia

83
CHAPTER 15
MR. PRESIDENT, HERE'S WHAT
YOU MISSED
Cass Lake Golf Club, Cass Lake

87
CHAPTER 16
ST PAUL'S "LAKE" MYSTERIES

93
CHAPTER 17
RUBIK WAS HERE

97
CHAPTER 18
THE HASTINGS BRIDGE
Valley View Golf Course, Hastings

103
CHAPTER 19
ANTIQUES QUIZ SHOW

109
CHAPTER 20
BACK TO THE '50S, AND A NAKED TRUTH
Albert Lea Country Club, Albert Lea

113
CHAPTER 21
UNHEARD OF
Orchard Beach and Golf Club, Lakeville

119
CHAPTER 22
CENTRAL HUB
St. Cloud Golf Club and others

127
CHAPTER 23
GREAT VIEW, TIGHT SQUEEZE
Riverdale Golf Course, Donehower/Dakota

137
CHAPTER 24
OUT OF BOUNDS? NOT REALLY.
Fountain City Golf Club, Fountain City, Wis.

142
CHAPTER 25
LOST GOLF COURSES: THE LIST

Introduction

THIS BOOK ISN'T SO MUCH A MULLIGAN
AS IT IS A SECOND SWING.

So here we go, second swing through Minnesota, on the hunt for lost golf courses.

Found one: Right there next to the Big River, I mean so on top of it you could putt out with one hand, walk across the road, and land a catfish with the other.

Found another: Up north, in lake country, home to hundreds of fish the size of that big channel cat. Thirtieth president of the United States passed on his chance to play it.

And another: Out west, in small-town Minnesota. But talk about history. The golf course was founded no less than a hundred years ago — PLUS TWENTY.

Found two others, veritable metro-area twins: The older, a convivial west-metro place with a hump running through it, how's that for a combination, that lived to be 98. The younger, on high ground to the east and with an inaugural name you've probably never heard of, that made it to 96.

Speaking of names you've never heard of, I'm betting you've not heard of half of these Minnesota golf courses. Put on your geography and history thinking caps, and you still won't have heard of half of them:

Castle Greens. Chain O'Lakes. Lake Park. McAllen. Riverdale. Silver Creek. Valley View. Wildwood.

Stumped? Or at least half-stumped? Read on.

More! Gone. delves into each of those disappearing acts, and more — 35 lost courses in narrative form, and 221 total in the all-time list.

It's all part of a second swing through Minnesota's lost golf courses, a follow-up to *Fore! Gone. Minnesota's Lost Golf Courses, 1897–1999*, published in 2014, 218 pages, same author, what a blast to research and write.

Ditto for *More! Gone.* The second effort covers some of the lost courses I have researched since 2015. Some, I have written about on my website, www.ForeGoneGolf.com. An additional dozen or so, I have researched in the past two years but not written about until now.

Before the second swing begins, a few swing tips:

- *More! Gone.*, like *Fore! Gone.* before it, does not indisputably cover every acre of lost-course ground in Minnesota history. Even with 221 lost courses identified, I am tap-in certain that there are scores more — maybe a hundred or more — resting in peace.

- My overriding interest since I started researching lost golf courses in 2010 has been on the long-lost, rather than the more recently departed. I've made a couple of exceptions this time around, but for me, it's still usually the older, the better.

- Printed ages of people mentioned in this book are as of the time I interviewed them. Sadly, some have since passed.

Now, time to swing away.

Joe Bissen

"One of the most fascinating things about golf is how it reflects the cycle of life. No matter what you shoot — the next day you have to go back to the first tee and begin all over again and make yourself into something."

— PETER JACOBSEN

CHAPTER 1
The Lefty is All Right

"He said,
'I think I broke a Guinness Book
of World Records.'"

More! Gone.

There is no recorded instruction that says you can't start a golf book with a story about a baseball player. I checked.

"Google, can I start a golf book with a story about a baseball player?"

Zero hits. A no-hitter. So play ball.

Jim Kaat, the former Minnesota Twins great, was a left-handed pitcher, a very good hitter at a position that requires not a whit of batting skill, and winner of a remarkable 16 Gold Gloves as the best-fielding pitcher in his league. So you know he was a great athlete.

On July 2, 1972, Kaat slid into second base in Chicago and broke his left wrist. His pitching season was over. His golf season was not. He spent much of the rest of summer and fall at Minnetonka Country Club in Shorewood, now a lost course.

"He had a cast put on so that the golf club would fit, and he played at Minnetonka," said Bob Olds, the former longtime pro at the club. "He played right-handed, and we became pretty good friends."

Some years later, Kaat phoned Olds.

"He said, 'I think I broke a Guinness Book of World Records. I shot my age this morning,'" Olds said. "I said, 'Yeah, well, you and 580 thousand other people.'

"He said, 'Yeah, but I shot my age again this afternoon.' I said, 'Now you're maybe down to probably 20 thousand.'

"He said, 'Yeah, but I did it right-handed in the morning and left-handed in the afternoon.'"

CHAPTER 2

Big Hitter, So to Speak

*"The day before he died,
he was making a trade with Dr. Nygren of Braham,
a dentist, for a set of new false teeth ..."*

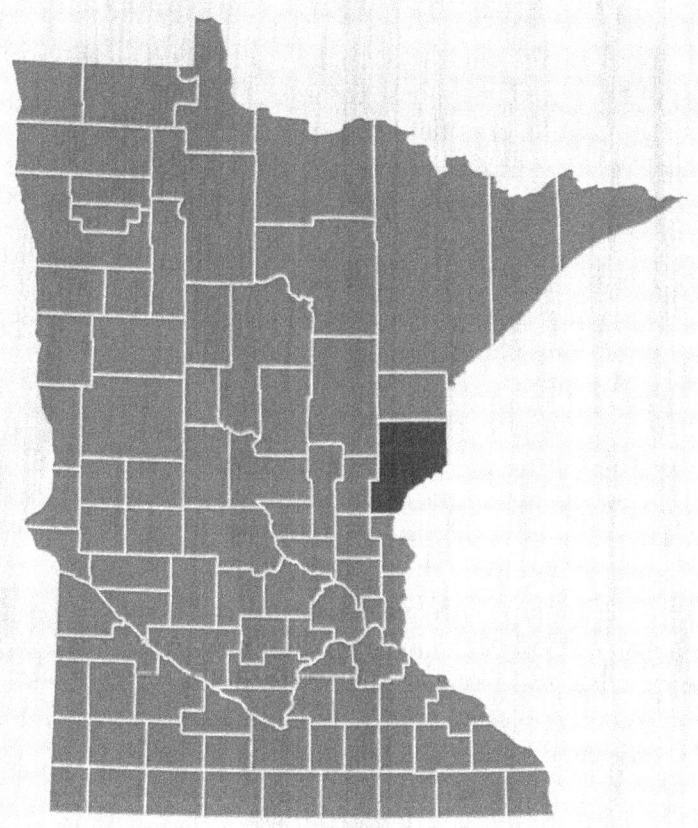

COURSE: MCALLEN GOLF COURSE
CITY: POKEGAMA TOWNSHIP
COUNTY: PINE
YEARS: 1931–CIRCA 1936

More! Gone.

G OLF WAS NOT A WAY OF LIFE FOR P.W. McALLEN, 1861–1942, HISTORICALLY NOTABLE RESIDENT OF PINE CITY, MINN. WHEELING AND DEALING WAS.

And what a set of wheels they were.

"He drove a 16-cylinder Cadillac ... big as a railroad train," remembered Pine City native Ben Boo, 94, the former mayor of Duluth, in a 2019 telephone interview.

McAllen's Cadillac often served to carry him back and forth between downtown Pine City, where he was vice president of the First State Bank of Pine County and did much of his wheeling-dealing, to his 300-plus-acre parcel alongside the western shore of Pokegama Lake, seven miles to the northwest via automobile.

A big-wheel McAllen anecdote:

"There was an auction sale out in our country," says a man in an audio recording held by the Pine City Area History Association, "and it was really muddy. (McAllen) got stuck in the driveway going into this farm. ... There was a bunch of farmers going up the driveway, walking, and he's spinnin' the wheels about 65 miles an hour, and this Caddy had big tires ... and these farmers including my dad got behind it, and he gunned it, and they were mud from one end to the other."

Speaking of "big as a railroad train," McAllen pretty much was. He stood at least 6 feet 7 and bore an ample girth, said one Pine Citian who remembered the man. Around this significant circumference, he at one time wore "a fine new unplucked otter coat," according to an account in the *Pine County Pioneer* newspaper from 1902.

Peter W. McAllen was a bank officer, creamery co-owner, poker player, racehorse owner (his Princess Patch was an offspring of the famed trotter Dan Patch), lumber and livestock trader ...

golf course owner ...

... boating enthusiast (in 1906, he introduced his vessel "The Knocker" to Pine County, top speed 17 mph), landlord, duck hunter, real estate investor and more.

"He was a godfather to the whole area out here," said Skip Pitzen, who called McAllen "Uncle Mac" and until his death at age 91 in December 2019 lived in a lakeside home on land once owned by McAllen.

P.W. McAllen
FROM STOFFEL FAMILY MEMORABILIA MUSEUM

Pitzen remembered McAllen's Caddy. The piston-powered behemoth was a convertible with a ragtop and was made to go places, just as the man himself was.

McAllen's farm — called a ranch by some who remember — was bordered on the west by County Highway 13 and on the east by 1,500-acre Pokegama Lake. To get from the highway to his property via motor vehicle, one had to cross a ditch. Across the ditch, McAllen built not a bridge or culvert (too easy) but rather a style, made of stone, upon which the Caddy went up and over so that McAllen wouldn't have to get out of his motorized monster and open or close a gate.

Within McAllen's property was his lakefront home, built in 1902 and set on a high point along the shore. Also on his land were two bath houses with water warmed by a tower exposed to the central Minnesota sun, as well as farmland, woods, a horse barn with half-mile racing track, and the nine-hole, sand-greens McAllen Golf Course.

"M'Allen Golf Course Opened Saturday," read a headline in the *Pine Poker* newspaper of June 4, 1931.

"The McAllen golf course opened last Saturday and 51 golfers were out to play on the new course," the story opened. "Thirty-eight played there Sunday. There were a number from the Twin cities, Duluth, Montevideo and other points, in addition to local folks, and they were all enthusiastic over the new course. The new course is a beauty and should eventually be one of the best in this section of the state."

Was it really a beauty? It's hard to say, 89 years later. The McAllen property today is mostly flat, although there is a now-thickly wooded area that the golf course probably was partly routed through. So there was promise in that respect. Plus, the Pokegama Lake backdrop certainly offered an aesthetic.

And then there was the promise relayed through a story in the *Pine County Pioneer* of June 12, 1931:

"This course was started last fall when preliminary ground work was done and the course laid out by Tom Vardon nationally known White Bear pro, who did a remarkable job, according to experts who have played around the course. A very unique feature is that every tee shot from each of the nine holes is made under a towering white pine tree, of from 75 to 100 feet high."

McAllen's golf course was a Vardon. That is not insignificant.

Tom Vardon was Minnesota's most notable golf course architect in the first half of the 20th century. An Englishman and the brother of six-time British Open champion Harry Vardon, he designed at least 40 courses in the Upper Midwest. He aided in the design of home-course White Bear Yacht Club, and his other designs or contributions include St. Cloud Country Club, Bolstad-University, Southview and Stillwater. (Fifteen miles to the north of Pokegama Lake lies another long-lost Vardon course. Read the next chapter. But finish this one first.)

The shortest hole on McAllen's course was 140 yards, the longest 530. McAllen was said to have been interested in having Minnesota Gov. Floyd B. Olson play there. There is no readily available evidence of whether that happened.

One day, McAllen and his banking and business partner, Fred Hodge, headed out to the course. At the time, McAllen was leasing part of his land to Henry Stoffel, who farmed it. Henry's son Ed, now 83, recalled what happened.

"My dad had bought a side rake for cutting hay," Ed Stoffel said in a 2019 interview. McAllen and Hodge came along, hitched up the rake and used it on the golf course. "They bent the teeth on it because they had set it so low," Stoffel added. "My dad was furious."

A side delivery rake owned by Henry Stoffel and "borrowed" by P.W. McAllen to mow his golf course. It is on site at the Stoffel Family Memorabilia Museum.

JOE BISSEN PHOTO

Weeks after Stoffel tells you this story, you visit his farm near Pine City, which features the Stoffel Family Memorabilia Museum, a barn-turned-trove of items from the Pine City area. Stoffel invites you out behind the barn — where Henry Stoffel's side rake, irresponsibly handled by Hodge and McAllen more than eight decades earlier, stands in retirement, tines still bent out of shape.

Stoffel noted, though, that McAllen also had an honorable side. On another visit, one of Hodge's dogs mauled the Stoffel family dog so badly that it had to be euthanized. Hodge apparently was unmoved, but McAllen, said Ed Stoffel, insisted that Hodge make amends, and so the Stoffels received $5, not a pittance at the time, as compensation.

For all of McAllen's entrepreneurial savvy, there is no evidence his Vardon-designed golf course ever took off — if, in fact, he even wanted it to. The consensus is that it was a private course, played only by invitation. A September 1931 story in the *Pioneer* reported that tournaments were being arranged with other golf clubs in the area, but there was no follow-up story. There was in fact scant coverage, period, of the McAllen Golf Course — a note in the *St. Cloud Times* of June 1932 mentioning that the course was open for the season, and a similar note in the April 1933 *Pine Poker*, but nothing else was found.

In Stoffel's museum, there is a *St. Paul Pioneer Press* story featuring a reprinted 1936 photo of McAllen and his longtime chauffeur, Vern Whiting, alongside a vehicle — Pitzen thought it was a Packard — that had been modified and turned into a "golfmobile" upon which McAllen navigated his golf course while in his 70s.

P.W. McAllen died of a heart attack at his Pokegama Lake farm home on Aug. 21, 1942. "Just the day before he died," his *Pine County Pioneer* obituary read, "he was making a trade with Dr. Nygren of Braham, a dentist, for a set of new false teeth in exchange for a horse he had at the farm. And we have been told on very authentic authority that he had only fibbed to Dr. Nygren ten years on the age of the animal. His sense of humor would have stood for this confession now, we are very sure."

PREQUEL

McAllen's nine-holer was not the first golf course in Pine City. In 1925, the *Pioneer* reported on a "temporary" course of seven holes to be built on fairgrounds land north of downtown Pine City. The Pine City Golf Links course opened on May 14, 1925, with Ben Boo, father of the Duluth mayor-to-be, as president. An old scorecard shows the course to have been 1,257 yards with a par of 22 and bogey of 27.

In April 1930, there was a report of a plan to add three more holes inside the fairgrounds race track. The presumption is existing holes would have been changed, making for a nine-hole course.

No mentions of the fairgrounds course beyond 1930 were found in the city's newspapers.

Almost two decades before that, however, golf apparently had made its way to the area in the form of a golf grounds on — insert drum roll — P.W. McAllen's Pokegama Lake farm.

In the Pine City Area History Association's holdings, there is a photo captioned "P.W. McAllen Farm & Golf Links, Pokegama Lake, Pine City, Minn." The association dates the photo to — and this would be remarkable if true — 1907.

Although I could find no mention of golf on McAllen's farm in the 1907 or 1908 issues of the *Pine Poker*, there also is no reason to doubt the veracity of the date on the photo. For one thing, the men and women pictured are wearing clothing typical of that period.

Best guess here is that McAllen had golf holes — but maybe not a formal

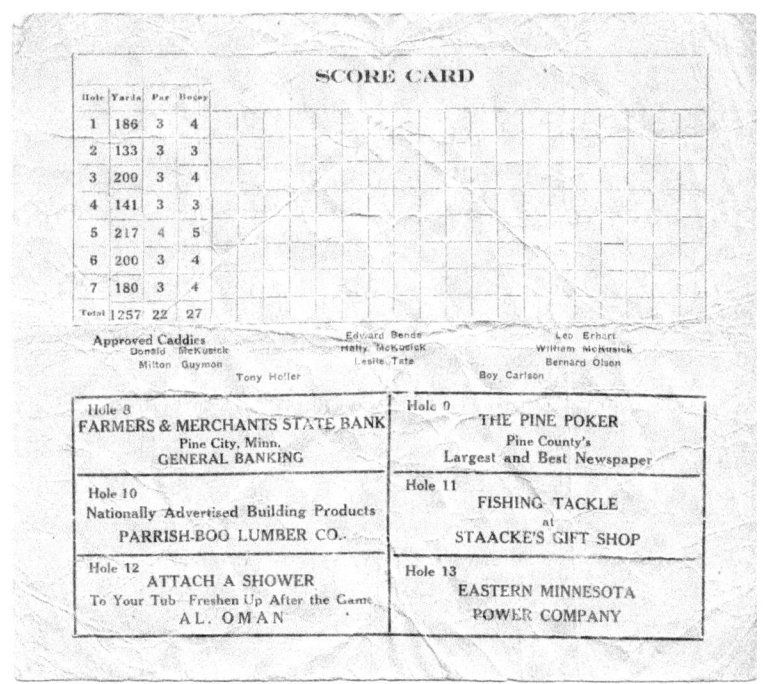

Scorecard from Pine City Golf Links course at the Pine City Fairgrounds.
COURTESY PINE CITY AREA HISTORY ASSOCIATION

Golf grounds on P.W. McAllen's Pokegama Lake ranch. Photo dated 1907.
HELD BY PINE CITY AREA HISTORY ASSOCIATION

course — on his property before 1931, when, noticing the burgeoning popularity of the game, he brought on Vardon and built a full-fledged nine-holer. But the 1907 date is significant, because to my knowledge, there were no golf grounds anywhere in east-central Minnesota — from Moose Lake to Foley to White Bear Lake — until the 1920 opening of the long-since-abandoned Chisago Golf Club in Chisago City.

CHAPTER 3

Tom and Tom Again

*"Eddy sank a ball
from about 100 yards,
the other day,
on the 4th hole."*

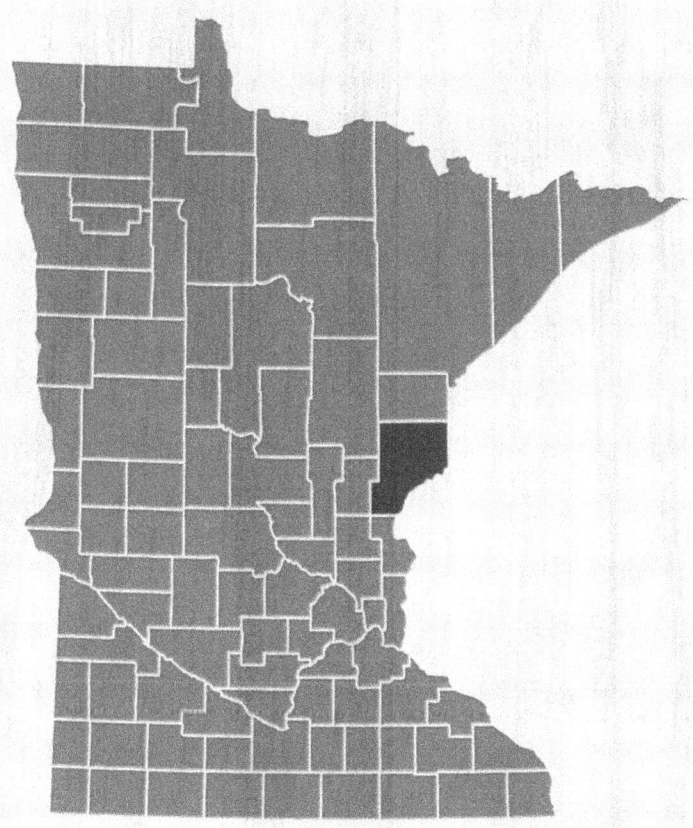

**COURSE: HINCKLEY GOLF COURSE
CITY: HINCKLEY
COUNTY: PINE
YEARS: 1929–36**

More! Gone.

Fourteen and a half miles north of P.W. McAllen's short-lived golf course near Pine City, Tom Vardon plied his trade on another plot of land at about the same time.

Taken together, it's hard to believe there could be a more obscure pair of Vardon courses anywhere, extant or extinct.

"The full nine holes of the Hinckley Golf Course are now ready for play," the *Hinckley News* reported on June 2, 1932, in a front-page "Golf Club Notes" column. "A large crew of men has been working for the past few weeks on the first four holes, and Pete Williams, under whose direction the work has been done, has announced that everything has been set for the opening.

"When the golf club was organized in 1929, Tom Vardon, noted pro and golf course architect from the White Bear Yacht Club, was asked to design it. Mr. Vardon was impressed with the amount of land given him on which to lay out a course and at the time he stated that of the many courses which he has designed, this was the largest tract. With the unlimited space on which to work he was able to layout a very sporting and lengthy course. We have over 3,000 yards which gives us the longest 9-hole course in this territory."

The column went on to report that four existing fairways had been plowed up and reseeded, and that the course

The site of Hinckley Golf Course, in east central Minnesota, today.
JOE BISSEN PHOTO

Tom Vardon, designer of Hinckley Golf Course and more than 40 other Midwest golf courses.
BAIN COLLECTION, LIBRARY OF CONGRESS

"has been made more attractive looking by the addition of new orange and black flags and racks." A 50-foot flagpole was erected near the clubhouse.

As implied, golf had been played on the land before Vardon's work was finished, but presumably not on a full nine-hole layout. On Sept. 11, 1930, the newspaper mentioned that a tournament would be played three days later, but "the golf club promises not to publish any but the winning score."

In what appears to have been the first Golf Notes column, published Sept. 28, 1930, it was reported that "AE Eddy sank a ball from about 100 yards, the other day, on the 4th hole."

The course lay 2.2 miles north of downtown Hinckley, between what is now County Highway 61 and the Willard Munger State Trail, formerly a railroad line. At the south end of the golf course land lies the property of Randy Rabe, who told me in 2019 that he found some old golf balls when the basement of his house was dug in 1980.

Hinckley Golf Course didn't last long. A shortstop tournament was played there in September 1933, with Joe "Pete" Williams beating 43 other entrants. In May 1935, the Eastern Minnesota Golf Association was formed, consisting of clubs from Hinckley, Sandstone, Rush City and North Branch. In June 1936, Hinckley golfers were invited to Sandstone's golf club for an open house. But I found no mention of a Hinckley golf club again later in 1936, '37 or '38.

THE VARDON LIST

In the previous chapter on P.W. McAllen's course, I noted that Vardon had designed at least 40 golf courses in the Upper Midwest. Which ones?

Below is a list, in chronological order and to the best of my knowledge, of Tom Vardon's design work. There are other Vardon lists on the Internet, but I am not aware of any with this many entries.

Settle Golf Club (North Yorkshire, England), 1895 (listed in golfclubatlas.com)

Austin Country Club, 1919

St. Cloud Country Club, 1919

Worthington Country Club, 1919

Meadow Lark Country Club (Great Falls, Mont.), 1919

St. Croix Valley Golf Club (St. Croix Falls, Wis.), 1920

Minnewaska Golf Club, Glenwood, 1920

Brainerd Country Club (later Pine Meadows, now defunct), 1921

Hillcrest Golf Club, St. Paul (lost course), 1921

Sauk Centre Country Club, 1921

Ortonville Golf Club (original nine, now a lost course), 1922

Amery Golf Club (Wis.), 1922

Matoska Country Club, Gem Lake (lost course), 1923

Stillwater Country Club (first nine), 1924

Lakeview Golf Club (Mitchell, S.D.), 1925

Quality Park, St. Paul (lost course), 1925

Clear Lake Golf Club (Wis.), 1926

Long Prairie Golf Club, 1927

St. James Golf Club, 1927

Cannon Glen Golf Club, Cannon Falls, 1926

Highland Park Golf Club, St. Paul, 1928 (likely the second nine)

Shoreland Golf Club, St. Peter, 1928

Lake City Golf Club, 1928

Southview Country Club, West St. Paul, 1928 (redesign)

Minot Country Club (N.D.), 1929 (with Clarence Haines)

Eau Claire Golf & Country Club (Wis.), 1929

Westwood Hills Golf Club, St. Louis Park (lost course), 1929

Hinckley Golf Course (lost course), 1929

University of Minnesota Golf Club, Falcon Heights, 1929 (redesign)

Spooner Golf Club (Wis.), 1930

Little Falls Golf Club, 1930–31 (redesign)

Merrill Golf Club (Wis.), 1930

Willmar Golf Club (now Eagle Creek), 1931

McAllen course, Pokegama Township, Pine County, 1931

Como Golf Club, St. Paul, 1932 (second nine)

Phalen Golf Club, St. Paul, 1932 (redesign)

Bunker Hills Country Club, Mendota Heights (lost course), 1933

Lee Park Golf Club (Aberdeen, S.D.), 1933

Rugby Golf Club (Rugby, N.D), 1934

Benson Golf Course, 1937 (likely a redesign)

Luck Golf Course (now Luck Municipal, Luck, Wis.), opened 1938

The others listed here are part of a Wikipedia entry. I will not deign to judge the veracity of "Wiki" listings. Judge for yourself:

Coventry Golf Club (England), 1911 (also credited by WorldGolf.com and golfclubatlas.com)

Kendal Golf Club (England) (alterations to the original layout)

St. Augustines (Cliffsend, England), 1907 (also credited by WorldGolf.com)

In addition, Wikipedia credits Vardon with adding pot bunkers to Strathpeffer (Scotland) Golf Club in 1908.

Contributions

White Bear Yacht Club — there is a long and sometimes-contentious thread about the original designer of WBYC at golfclubatlas.com. Essentially, one camp considers Donald Ross the primary designer; another believes William Watson was the original designer. Either way, it is apparent that Vardon contributed to the lauded design.

Shattuck Golf Course (Faribault; it now is what I termed in *"Fore! Gone."* a "rebirthed" course — the Shattuck course is gone, replaced in its entirety on the same site by Legacy Golf Course)

CHAPTER 4

Three Courses, Two Golfers, One Good Sport

"Harm Snook of Luverne dropped 24 balls into the river and won seven new balls and a fishing net to get back his old ones."

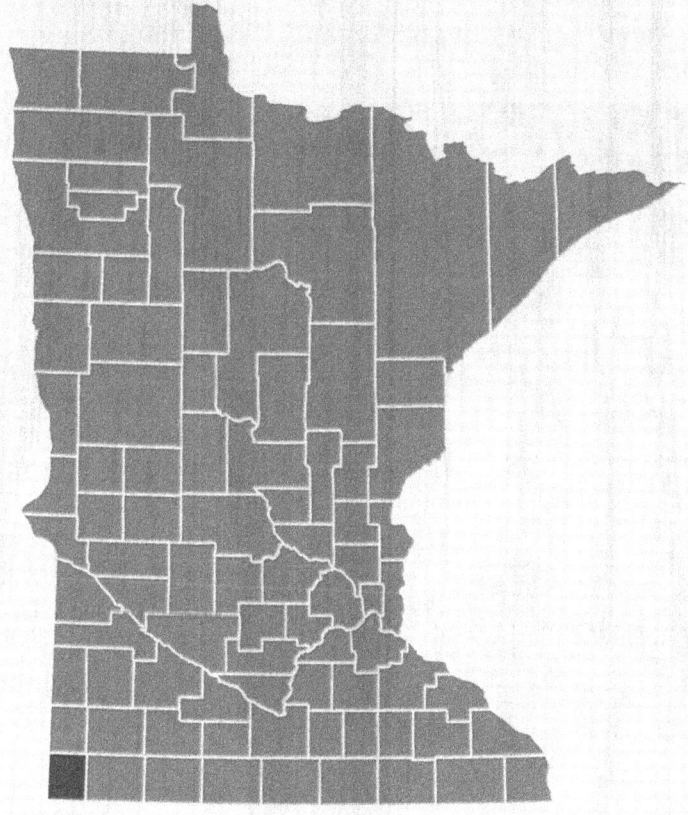

COURSES: LUVERNE GOLF CLUB
(GABRIELSON/PRESTON FARM AND ROCK RIVER)
CITY: LUVERNE
COUNTY: ROCK
YEARS: 1925–38

More! Gone.

BEFORE GOLF IN LUVERNE, MINN., HAD JERILYN BRITZ, IT HAD LUVERNE COUNTRY CLUB, TWO OTHER GOLF COURSES AND DON SPEASE.

Connecting the dots, that makes over 95 years' worth of golf in Luverne.

Jerilyn Britz's golf tale is well-known and oft-documented. As a teenager in Luverne, a city of 4,000 in the southwestern corner of Minnesota, she showed an aptitude for many sports but had not played golf until, while working as a lifeguard at the municipal pool in 1960, she received a push — but not into the water — from the pool manager, Charles Weinman.

Jerilyn Britz is one of the top names in Minnesota golf history, with a U.S. Women's Open championship and one other LPGA Tour victory to her credit.

COURTESY MINNESOTA STATE MANKATO ATHLETICS

"He would come down every day and start talking about golf and tell stories about things that happened" on the course, Britz said by phone in January 2018. Weinman persuaded Britz to pick up a club and take a few whacks at dandelions, and she soon began backswinging and downswinging with golf balls in the way. She was hooked.

"I hit one good shot and have tried to have that feeling ever since," she said. "It was such a different feeling."

Britz joined Luverne Country Club, won four club championships in the 1960s and turned professional at age 30. In July 1979, she participated in a little four-day soiree' at Brooklawn Country Club in Fairfield, Conn., known as the U.S. Women's Open, where she shot rounds of 70, 70, 75 and 69 to earn the title of national champion golfer of the year. It was the first of her two tournament championships in more than 20 years on the LPGA Tour, and she was named to the Minnesota Golf Hall of Fame in 2007. She also was the first woman named to the Rock County Historical Society's Hall of Fame. As of 2019, she continued to play events with famed fellow competitors on the Legends Tour.

Which brings us, quite indirectly, to Don Spease and another memorable round of golf, almost exactly 30 years before Britz's string of four in 1979.

But a round of a decidedly different ilk.

"Records were broken in more than one department Friday when Minnehaha Country Club held its annual invitational golf tournament," the *Argus-Leader* of Sioux Falls, S.D., reported on Aug. 27, 1949.

This event wasn't so much a golf tournament as it was a dawn-to-darkness marathon that featured a colossal field of 301 golfers and 150 door prizes.

"... there were some 1600 dollars of prizes awarded," the newspaper continued, "more than in any previous tournament ...

"... and possibly the 187 total score Don Spease of Luverne turned in is the highest round yet to be admitted to."

Yes, that would be 187 strokes for 18 holes — pushing 100 per nine.

Spease that day could not master either the art of clearing water hazards or getting the ball in the hole. "It's almost certain," the *Argus-Leader* added, "that Spease' 78 putts are pretty much of a mark. For his prodigious efforts the Luverne man won an auto spotlight and (really) a putter."

Boyd Barrett was the skilled Luverne outlier in that tournament, shooting a 77 that landed him in second place. But others from across the border were hot on Spease's tail.

"Luverne had the monopoly on high scores," the *Argus-Leader* reported, "with Bob Lundberg joining Spease in that department by virtue of 19 strokes on one hole. Golf shoes are now his as a result.

"Harm Snook of Luverne dropped 24 balls into the river and won seven new balls and a fishing net to get back his old ones. Jim Sherman, also of Luverne, sank 14 and received a cap and four balls."

Luverne didn't have the market cornered on deposits into the Big Sioux River that day. "Cliff Chamley of Flandreau (S.D.) and E.P. Fortner of Mitchell dropped 11 and 10" balls into the river, the newspaper continued.

If you're counting, and there's no reason you should be, that's 59 balls in the water from one set of four hapless hackers.

More than 68 years after his fateful foray into Sioux Falls, I dialed Spease's phone number to see if he remembered his Minnehaha round or had any objections to a retelling.

On the other end of the line, Spease laughed.

"Yes, I remember," he said — then offered the perfect caveat.

He had never golfed before that day.

Spease said he had traveled the 15 miles from Luverne to Minnehaha with his cousin and a couple of friends mostly so the others could meet the tournament requirement of having a foursome to play. He was 16 years old.

"I played basketball and football," said Spease, now 85. "They had to have a foursome, so they asked if I would go along. I said, 'I don't know anything about golf,' but I went along."

Once on the course, it quickly became evident that he was no match for Minnehaha CC and the Big Sioux.

"They gave me four balls to play with," Spease said. "After the first two holes, I had lost two of the four balls in the river. So after that, when I got close to the river, they let me throw my ball across the river."

Spease confirmed the report of his prize winnings. The auto spotlight went on his 1935 Ford. The putter was sold to a friend's mother for $10. "That was a lot of money back then," he said.

Finding competitive golf to not be in his athletic wheelhouse, Spease did not play again for many years. He worked in his family's tire business in Luverne and at other jobs, has retired four times, he says, and boasts an ample record of volunteer and community service.

None of this has the first thing to do with lost golf courses, does it? But it is one doozy of a back story.

On to business. Britz mailed me a copy of Luverne Country Club's eight-page 50th anniversary pamphlet, published in 1989. One entry is a recounting titled "History of the golf course."

"There were two golf courses in Luverne before the present course was developed," the tale begins. "The first course was west of town on the site of the Gordon Gabrielson farm. It was a 9-hole layout, even with a water hole, on which some members used floater balls. … The second course was located three miles south and a half mile east of Luverne along the Rock River. It also was nine holes. This course lasted only a few seasons. It crossed the river several times and each spring it seemed the swinging bridges would wash away, and the mosquitos were so fierce they decided to abandon it. It was then in 1939 the course was moved east of Luverne on what was called the old Fogg Estate. Here is where the course has been for the last 50 years."

Officially, golf in Luverne dates to April 23, 1925, when "permanent organization of the Luverne Golf club was completed," the *Rock County Star* reported the next day. J.M. Rustad was the first president. Membership was to be limited to 100, with an impressive inaugural class of more than 80 signed up. The course would be established through a one-year lease on the 80-acre Charles Preston farm, 3.5 miles almost directly west of downtown Luverne and immediately south of County Highway 5. (A Gabrielson family, referenced in the previous paragraph, owned the 240 acres to the south of the Preston farm, according to plat maps of the day.)

Luverne golfers played in tournaments at places like Worthington, 30 miles to the east, and staged competitions at their own club. Carl Schmuck won with a 71 in May 1929, and Perry A. Arnette, "Harmonica King and farmer," according to the newspaper, was runner-up with a 75.

Arnette was a central figure in early Luverne golf. He served as Luverne GC president during the late 1920s, and in August 1931, plans were announced for Luverne Golf Club to move to the Rock River site, on land owned by Arnette.

This was thought to be a site of great potential. The course was to be laid out by Frank Brokl, the 1929 Minnesota State Amateur champion from Minneapolis who specialized in designing small-town courses across Minnesota, South Dakota and Iowa, including now-lost courses at Lake Benton and Ivanhoe. The sand greens were to be 50 feet in diameter, the *Rock County Herald* reported, and the parcel was highly touted by the newspaper.

"Among the numerous advantages of the new grounds are scattered clusters of trees which shade some of the holes, the substantial grass growth and heavy sod; the natural hazard of the Rock River, which must be crossed twice

Three Courses, Two Golfers, One Good Sport

Undated postcard from The L.L. Cook Company of a Luverne golf course. Best guess is that this was at the Rock River site, based mostly on the sand green (note how perfectly round it is).

while following the course, and the fact that a player must face the sun only on the first hole."

The *Herald* story said the new grounds would not be put into play until spring of 1932 and that, in order to keep the grass closely cropped, "a flock of sheep will be pastured on the links."

Once the Rock River site opened, it lasted through 1938. In July 1934, Luverne hosted a "Tri-State tournament," the *Minneapolis Tribune* reported. "The Luverne course is 2,881 yards long and supplied with many natural beauty spots and hazards," the story read.

It seems likely the club underestimated the Rock River's capacity for breaching its banks and making golf a muddy mess. Beyond the Luverne CC pamphlet, two others I talked with confirmed that flooding can be a problem in that area.

There certainly are few remaining bridges between the Rock River site and the current Luverne Country Club site east of town. One of them, coincidentally, is named Don Spease.

Spease remembered the Rock River site. "My dad used to go out and play golf there. I'd go along," he said. "The course had sand greens. My job was to drag a piece of rope with heavy carpet so they could putt."

Luverne GC abandoned the Rock River site and relocated two miles east of downtown for the 1939 season, eventually taking the name Luverne Country Club. An *Argus-Leader* story noted that the new course would open on May 14 with all greens ready and one day of free play for all. P.M. Conner was club president.

Britz, who now lives in Florida, loves the tree-lined layout at the current Luverne Country Club. She appreciates sunsets from the eighth tee, where, she says, one can see all the way to Iowa and South Dakota. "I've played golf all over the world," she said. "I don't think I have ever played a course as fun as Luverne."

More! Gone.

It's tough to say whether Don Spease would say the same. He began golfing again in his 50s at Luverne CC and was a far more respectable player than during his Minnehaha day, with scores in the 50s for nine holes. Then fate intervened again.

"The last year I played golf out there, the first round of season, I was riding in a three-wheel cart," Spease recalled, again summoning his sense of humor. The driver of the cart swerved to avoid a tree root, and Spease stuck his leg out of the cart to keep his balance.

"I broke my ankle," he said.

Spease has not played the game again.

Golf in Luverne lives on.

CHAPTER 5
Tough Times

"During the war, you couldn't get no golf balls, couldn't get no clubs. They were making bullets."

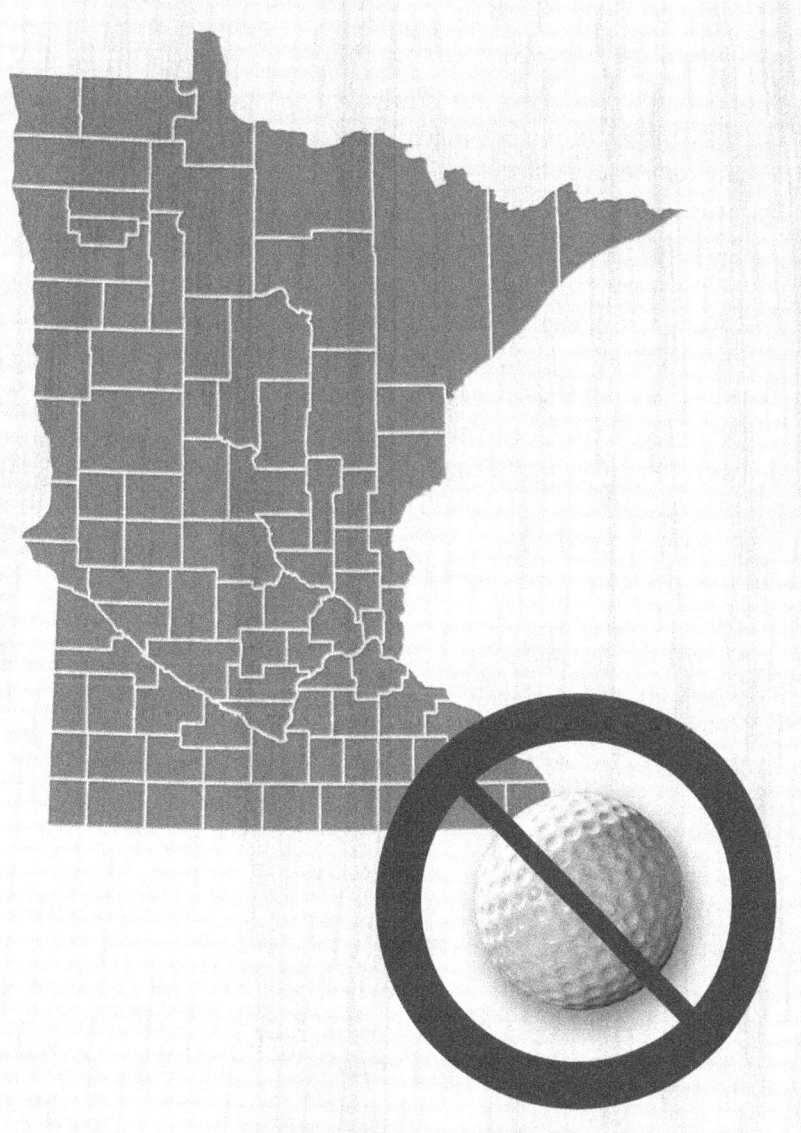

More! Gone.

Minnesota's lost golf courses lie in permanent repose near every border of the state, from Luverne to Moorhead to Warroad to Bayport, and in scores of places within. But when were they born? And why did they die?

There are a hundred answers to those questions. The first lost course, Winona Golf Club, was born in 1897. The last ... well, this phenomenon is in its 124th year. Some lost courses looked like well-groomed, verdant expanses. Others looked like, well, Farmer Farmall's back 40, which they often were. They died because of hard times. They died because higher powers — city or state authorities, anyway — wanted the land. And they died because selling to a real estate developer made a lot more dollars and sense than continuing to run a golf course.

Still, with all that said, there is one distinct, unmistakable pattern among Minnesota's earlier lost golf courses. It is so uncannily common that it is almost a template:

Born during good times of the 1920s. Expired during gloomier days of the '30s and '40s.

(There also is a pattern, to be perfectly accurate, among latter-day lost courses: Born in the 1990s and very early 2000s, gone by 2020. As of April 2020, 75 Minnesota courses fit this era's supply-exceeded-demand template. However, I have far less appetite for rehashing those stories than the earlier ones.)

A step back in time for the early lost courses is required here. Remember the WABAC Machine from "The Rocky and Bullwinkle Show"? Crank it up, Peabody and Sherman.

The year is 1920. The United States has weathered the latter half of a decade in which a world war claimed 8.5 million lives worldwide and a Spanish influenza pandemic claimed almost 30 million more. After a brief economic depression in 1920 and 1921, America picks up steam like a runaway locomotive. The byword for the new decade is "prosperity."

Radios, refrigerators and ranges appear in Americans' homes. More and more Model-T's appear on their driveways, giving Americans never-before-imagined access to places near and far. As the decade advances, most people have more money. In 1920, the average income for a Minnesota wage earner is $2,940. By 1927, that figure will rise to $4,812.

The good times are rolling, and they are rolling right into the growing game of golf. Newspapers and magazines trumpet the achievements of the game's great players, including the consummate gentleman Bob Jones and the consummate swashbuckler Walter Hagen. The American public is enamored of the game, and to sate the thirst, golf courses are built. Everywhere.

"By the 1920s," Minnesota author Rick Shefchik wrote in *From Fields to Fairways*, a fabulous compendium of Minnesota's classic golf clubs, "golf had become so popular and fashionable that no self-respecting community of any size wanted to be without a course of its own ..."

No kidding. Only seven Minnesota courses were listed in the 1916 *American Annual Golf Guide*. By 1926, the same guide listed 75 Minnesota courses. The year before, the book *Tee Party on the Green* had reported 82 Minnesota courses, ranking 14th in the nation.

But a five-day span in late October 1929 changed everything.

The morning of Oct. 24, 1929 — "Black Thursday" — opened a mass sell-off on Wall Street and precipitated a cataclysmic stock market crash. By the time sunset arrived five days later, on Black Tuesday, Wall Street had been reduced to a figurative pile of rubble. According to one estimate, the value of U.S. stocks dropped by $16 billion over the final months of 1929.

Soon, the nation was plunged into the Great Depression. By 1933, the U.S. unemployment rate had reached 25 percent. In 1934, the Minnesota unemployment rate was 22 percent. Thousands of Americans took to government bread lines just to eat. Personal income dropped by 50 percent. Crop prices dropped by 60 percent.

Farms failed. Banks failed. So did golf courses.

Golf courses, to be blunt, dropped like flies in the 1930s and 1940s. Almost 60 are known to have expired in one of those two decades. It's more likely that at least 100 did.

Down they went, like tomato cans against Joe Louis. First, construction slowed considerably. Through the 1920s, the Minnesota golf magazine *The 10,000 Lakes Golfer* included nearly ceaseless reports or updates on new-course construction in Minnesota. By 1932, similar reports in the magazine's successor, *The Amateur Golfer & Outdoor Magazine*, had vanished. By 1936, only 36 courses remained on the Minnesota Golf Association's roster of member courses.

How tough were those times? The website of Jackson Golf Club, in southwestern Minnesota, reports that the club's cash on hand at the end of 1931 was $1.73.

Private courses, because they tended to have backers with deep financial pockets, bobbed and weaved and generally survived the Great Depression. Northwood Country Club in North St. Paul, now a lost course, was one such example. Almost all of the other lost courses of that era were municipally owned, daily-fee or semi-private.

The summer of 1936 produced another blow — a scalding one. The Great Heat Wave of 1936 was both extraordinary and deadly. The temperature peaked at 106 in Duluth, 108 in Minneapolis and 114 in Moorhead, an all-time high in the state. Grasshoppers were fried alive in farmers' fields. There was a human toll as well: Over a 15-day period in July, nearly 800 Minnesotans were reported to have died from the heat. In a nine-day period early in the month, the heat wave killed 240 people in St. Paul, according to a 1936 *White Bear Press* story.

Though there is no direct evidence the 1936 heat wave contributed to the demise of any golf courses, it couldn't have helped any of them.

"Everything was burned," remembered the late Mike Rak, an outstanding player at the lost Hilltop Public Golf Links course in Columbia Heights.

Amid unprecedented hard times for golf courses, a shot in the arm finally came on Dec. 17, 1936, with the announcement that $10.5 million in relief funds would be spent on new and existing golf courses through President Franklin D. Roosevelt's Works Progress Administration. WPA projects put unemployed Americans back on the job — many of them on the golf course.

Sports Illustrated noted in a 2009 story that the WPA and Civil Works Administration built or renovated nearly 600 municipal golf courses in the United States. Among the WPA projects in Minnesota: a clubhouse and pro shop at Keller in Maplewood, five new greens at Columbia in Minneapolis, and at least a dozen new-course projects statewide. WPA contributed to at least one course going "lost," as well: With WPA help, Ortonville Golf Club moved its club from north of town to a superior location overlooking Big Stone Lake.

But not every ailing golf course received WPA elixir, and more Minnesota courses passed into oblivion in the late 1930s.

Then, one more sledgehammer's blow for American golf: U.S. entry into World War II in December 1941. The war put 16.1 million Americans in military uniforms. More than 15½ million of those were men, and when it's considered that golf still was largely a game played by men in the early 1940s, that translates to a huge loss in numbers of people on hand to pony up a daily greens fee.

Al Schultz, late mayor of Bayport, estimated in 2012 that 50 percent of that city's males enlisted in World War II. The late "Peanuts" Bell, who caddied and played at the lost course in Bayport, was one of them, having served in the 15th Air Force in Italy. In fact, the vast majority of men who were interviewed for *"Fore! Gone."* and who remembered lost golf courses of the 1930s and '40s were World War II veterans. Rak served in the Army's 91st Infantry in Africa. The late Don Dostert (Bunker Hills) served with the 1st Marines in the Pacific. Bud Chapman (Westwood Hills) flew B-29s. The late John Burton (The Minnetonka Club) served with the Navy in the Mediterranean. The late Thor Nordwall (Matoska) served with the Army Signal Corps in Europe.

While the men were away, the women did not play — golf, nor much of anything else. American citizens were singularly focused on the war effort. Government policies underlined those efforts. On Dec. 17, 1941, the Office of Price Administration ordered an 80 percent reduction in the production of new golf balls. On April 9, 1942, the War Production Board ordered a complete stop to the manufacturing of golf equipment as of May 31, 1942. That edict was eased the next month, when the WPB permitted clubs to be manufactured with material already on hand.

Those who oversaw golf responded in kind. On Jan. 11, 1942, the United States Golf Association canceled all of its championships for the duration of the war. The 1943 PGA Tour season consisted of only three events. Augusta National closed in 1943 for the duration of the war, and the club allowed 50 cows to graze its property.

In the words of the late Frank Fiorito, a longtime St. Paul-area golf professional: "During the war, you couldn't get no golf balls, couldn't get no clubs. They were making bullets."

The war's momentum turned by 1944, and in 1945, it concluded in victory for the Allies. America suffered more than 400,000 casualties (dead or missing), and thousands more came home seriously injured. Comparatively, the war's cost on the game of golf was, of course, a pittance. Still, it was real. More Minnesota courses folded during the war years or shortly after — Hilltop in Columbia Heights and Bunker Hills in Mendota Heights, to name just two.

Postwar, America recovered. So did its golf courses, as the game enjoyed a period of expansion — thank you, Sam, Patty, Ben, Arnie, Jack, Lee, Gary, Tom, Nancy, Shark, Freddie, Annika and Tiger — that lasted nearly 50 years.

But for the lost golf courses of the 1930s and 1940s, almost nothing remained, except for faded memories.

A version of this chapter appeared in Fore! Gone.

CHAPTER 6
Oui, Je Crois Je L'avoir Trouvé

"Phillip also played hard during his lifetime, and had a very good singing voice. After a few drinks of Blue Ribbon Whiskey he could be quite an entertainer. ..."

COURSE: RED LAKE FALLS GOLF CLUB
CITY: RED LAKE FALLS
COUNTY: RED LAKE
YEARS: 1930–1932

More! Gone.

Is there a city in Minnesota with a more distinct French accent than Red Lake Falls?

Maybe, but pour l'amour de Dieu (for goodness' sake), this place is something.

Allow me, then, to translate the title of this chapter. It reads, if my English-to-French translator is not on the fritz, "Yes, I believe I have found it."

Why the bilingual mumbo-jumbo? It's intended to be a tribute to the French heritage emanating from Red Lake Falls, a northwestern Minnesota city of 1,400 in Red Lake County, 35 miles east of Grand Forks, N.D.

Red Lake Falls' French roots run deeper than those laid down by the hardwoods spreading along the banks of the two rivers, Red Lake and Clearwater, that wind through the area. Red Lake Falls has a Champagne Avenue and a Langevin Avenue and a Bottineau Avenue. (Even the word "avenue" is of French origin.) All that's missing is an Arc de Triomphe replica at the intersection of International and Champagne avenues. No, I'm not suggesting they build one.

The local campground in Red Lake Falls is named Voyageur's View. The motel on Minnesota Highway 32 is the Chateau. They serve French fries (yeah, cheap joke) at Joe DiMaggio's, the restaurant on the south side of town — though I have to nitpick here. If you were going to name a Red Lake Falls sports bar after a baseball Hall of Famer, why not Napoleon Lajoie, "The Frenchman," 1896–1916, .338 career batting average?

Red Lake Falls' founding speaks to its roots. In 1798, French Canadian trader Jean Baptiste Cadotte established a trading post at what is now Sportsman Park. The city's better-known pioneer was a French-American named Pierre Bottineau. In 1876, he led a group of French-Americans northwest from Ramsey and Hennepin counties; they homesteaded the area and were joined two years later by a colony of French settlers from upper Canada.

Today, much of the French heritage remains. Plat maps and telephone directories are chock-full of names of French origin. Red Lake Falls couldn't be more French-connected if its high school were named Lafayette.

Which, of course, it is.

None of this, of course, has the first thing to do with golf, unless one were to point out that some scholars of the game posit that a form of the "Scottish game"

was played in, yes, France, Belgium and the Netherlands as early as the 15th century. But there is a connection, if only tangential, between golf in Red Lake Falls and the land of croissants and Bordeaux.

The city's long-established golf course is Oak Knolls, a nine-hole layout along the Clearwater River on the southeast side of town. Many websites list 1940 as Oak Knolls' date of establishment. That is true, but only in a kinda-sorta-not-the-whole-story way.

The *Red Lake Falls Gazette* of April 11, 1940, suggested golf had already been played in Red Lake Falls, reporting that the city's golf club was about to be reorganized. The next week's paper confirmed it. "Pierre Bottineau Golf Club Is Re-Organized," the headline read. The golf course, it turned out, had "reverted back to nature" in recent years but was about to be revived on the same site — the one on the Clearwater River, same as its present-day site.

But in fact, golf on the Clearwater site predated 1940. And golf in Red Lake Falls went back even further.

Take it from a *Minneapolis Tribune* story of April 24, 1932. "The golf course at the new Red Lake Falls park has been reseeded and will be ready for play early in June, according to President Guy F. Hennings," the *Tribune* reported. "More than 400 pounds of seed, mixture of blue grass and red top and clover, was spread over the entire six-hole course. The old course at the Phil Demarais farm will be used until the new one is fit for play."

Demarais. Another classic name of French origin. And there's your lost golf course. On the Phil Demarais farm. Wherever that was.

Time to put on the thinking beret and find the lost course.

Phil's Farm

Sometimes, pinpointing the site of a lost golf course takes less time than it takes to play a round of mini-golf. The lost course might be described in detail in an old newspaper story, or the first person you call happens to remember the eagle he made on the par–5 eighth in 1942 ("drove it past the silo on the right, grabbed my cleek, lofted it over the herd of sheep on the left and knocked in a 40-footer with my trusty MacGregor").

And sometimes, Phil Demarais.

Tracking down the Demarais farm/lost golf course was not easy. Circling the area via an old aerial photo revealed nothing. An initial look at old plat maps, ditto. A phone inquiry connected with a woman who had been born a Demarais. She offered a pronunciation of the name in those parts (DEM-uh-ruh) and suggested one might look near Terrebonne ("good earth" in French), a township and former town site southeast of Red Lake Falls. There was nothing in Terrebonne plat maps, though, except more French names that weren't Demarais: Cadieux, Sauve, Laframboise and dozens of others.

Nothing showed promise until a relatively deep search for Phil Demarais background on the Internet. Finally — please excuse moi for another Francophone reference — voila!

Mr. Demarais was quite the notable character.

Phillip Demarais, born in 1874 in Weedon, Quebec, was the son of Red Lake County pioneer John Baptiste Desmarais I, according to an entry in the geneaology web site RootsWeb, citing an entry in *A History of Red Lake County*. (Other websites also note different spellings of the surname; it seems possible Phillip dropped the first "s.") He lived and farmed in Pleasant Lake Township, the web site entry read.

"Phillip loved to dance and would often call the squares at the neighborhood dances. He played the mouth harp and could even bang a good rhythm on a common dish pan."

The Gazette story continued: "Phillip also played hard during his lifetime and had a very good singing voice. After a few drinks of Blue Ribbon Whiskey he could be quite an entertainer. ...

"He was known in the area as a man who was always there when someone needed help, especially around butchering time because he could make salt pork better than anyone."

All that aside, I still wanted most to find out where his farm was, and where the lost golf course lay.

The notation that Demarais' farm was in Pleasant Lake Township (more commonly referred to as Lake Pleasant Township) sent me back to the Red Lake County plat maps. And there it was. Maps from 1911 and 1916 both show plots owned by either/and/or "Philip Desmarais," Delina Desmarais (Phillip's first wife) and D. Desmarais at the very northeastern corner of Lake Pleasant Township, 3.2 miles southeast of downtown Red Lake Falls and adjacent to Terrebonne Township on the east. In current terms, the farm was at the southwest corner of the intersection of county roads 114 and 115.

Oui, je crois je l'avoir trouvé.

The Demarais golf course likely was the first one in Red Lake Falls. A *Gazette* story from May 1, 1930, reported that the city's golfers were organizing and planned to build a course on the Demarais farm. Beyond that, I know little about the course — number of holes, length of course, etc. The Demarais plot was mostly flat, sharply rectangular, and bisected by Lower Badger Creek. I later learned from John Thibert, president of the Red Lake County Historical Society, that such a layout was a French staple — they typically would divide sections of land in rectangular fashion so as to afford as many residents as possible access to a waterway and with a house nearby.

By now, you shouldn't be surprised by some of the names of the folks who owned land near the Demarais farm: Ducharme, Champeau, Quesnell, Gagnon, Robillard, Latendress ... you get the idea.

The golf course on the Demarais plot was abandoned in 1932, according to the aforementioned *Minneapolis Tribune* story. Demarais sold the farm in 1936, according to the Gazette story, "semi-retired," and bought and operated a grocery store in nearby Brooks before selling again and moving to Terrebonne, near one of his favorite fishing holes. When he died in 1952 of tuberculosis in Thief River Falls, he was, according to one Internet entry, the last surviving pioneer settler in Red Lake County.

Golf in Red Lake Falls lived on after moving off the Demarais property and onto the current Oak Knolls site. In April 1932, committees were chosen for the six-hole Red Lake Falls Golf Club, with Otto F. Hennings as president and memberships costing $10. M.E. Jones, an engineer with the state highway department, presented a sketch of the golf course. Three additional holes along the bend of the Clearwater River were not to be put into play until 1933.

It took until mid-1932 for the course to be playable. The *Gazette* reported on

July 28 that the course at Bottineau park was now open, employing six sand greens and supported by 33 members.

"Some of the local golfers who have played the course and have lost a goodly number of balls complain the course is too sporty," the newspaper reported. "Others who make the rounds and return with more golf balls than when they started say it isn't sporty enough. The truth probably lies between those two extremes and the bulk of the players say it is going to be just right."

Though I did not scour every issue of the *Gazette* through the rest of the 1930s, what I did scan revealed no more signs of golf in Red Lake Falls until April 1940, with the mention of the club, now named Pierre Bottineau, having reorganized after the previous period of inactivity.

The course's name at some point was changed from Bottineau to Oak Knolls, and it exists today as a nine-holer with grass greens. "You will be challenged to keep your ball dry as a small stream, the pond, or the river entices your ball to take a dip," reads a passage on redlakefallsgolf.com.

Carry on, Red Lake Falls golfers. Au revoir, Monsieur Demarais.

CHAPTER 7

Comfort Zone

"(Club members) are still mourning the fact that they don't have Minnetonka Country Club anymore and how much they miss the whole experience. It was just an awesome place."

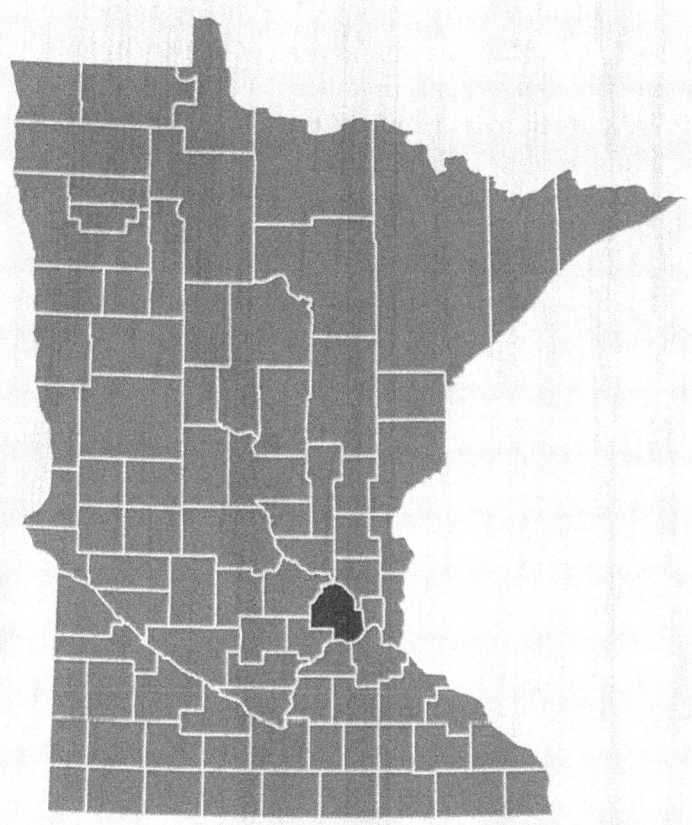

COURSE: MINNETONKA COUNTRY CLUB
CITY: SHOREWOOD
COUNTY: HENNEPIN
YEARS: 1916–2014

More! Gone.

BOB OLDS WAS NAME-DROPPING, BUT NOT FOR NAME-DROPPING'S SAKE.

"Nancy took care of her. Patty was not in very good health then," Olds said from his Minnetonka home in October 2019. "She was lying down on the couch in the ladies locker room and Nancy came in and said, 'What can I help you with?'"

Just to shift the Club Car into reverse for a moment, here are your aforementioned principals: Olds, a Minnesota Golf Association Hall of Fame member and for 39 years the pro at Minnetonka Country Club; his wife, Nancy; and Patty, a charming, by-then-older woman from Minneapolis of some golfing repute — last name of Berg.

Correct — Patty Berg, 15-time women's major champion and the first president of the Ladies Professional Golf Association. The year is uncertain, but Berg was conducting a clinic at Minnetonka CC.

"She wanted some water," Olds continued. "She was going to do a clinic off the first tee. And we must have had 500 people there. ... I went and said, 'Miss Berg' — she said, 'It's Patty'— and I said, Patty, are you ready, can you do this?

"It was raining, not very hard, just sprinkling, and we had bleachers set up around the first tee and all these people around there with their rainsuits on and everything to watch this, and I said, 'I've got an umbrella and I'll walk you down to the tee.

"I had a Ben Hogan umbrella — she played for Wilson, and I said, 'I'm sorry; I don't have a Wilson,' and she said, 'That's OK, Ben owes me a lot anyway.' We walked down to the first tee and (she) was kind of tottering, and she gets down to this area — it was like she was 25 years old, she walked in and said, 'Hey, everybody, how's it going,' and everybody said, we're sorry it's raining, and she said, 'Ah, baloney, I've won tournaments in the rain,' and she said forget about that.

"She hit shots to a kid out there in the first fairway — draw, fade; this kid (on the range) was picking up balls right there where she hit driver. She could still play to hit it like that. Jokes, funny things, really interesting."

Berg went on to complete the clinic. Born in 1918, she left us in 2006 at age 88, after 45 LPGA Tour victories and induction into the World Golf Hall of Fame. It was a heck of a run.

Ditto for Minnetonka Country Club, born 1916, departed 2014, age 98.

Honestly, Olds really wasn't on a name-dropping mission. If he had been, it might have gone something like this:

Jerry Barber, Patty Berg, Les Bolstad, Joan Garvin, Joel Goldstrand, Lisa Grimes, Nancy Harris, multiple Herrons, Jimmy Johnston, Willie Kidd, Tom Lehman, Marilyn Lovander, Barbara Moxness, Chi Chi Rodriguez, Bob Rosburg, Dick and Pat Sawyer, Curtis Strange, Bev Vanstrum, Lanny Wadkins, Anne Zahn, Fuzzy Zoeller.

And a good hundred or so others.

All of the above — legends of Minnesota golf and/or stars on pro circuits — played in tournaments or exhibitions at Minnetonka Country Club. Yet name-dropping does not capture the essence of what the club was.

"I just remember the people that worked there were awesome ... the cooks, the help, the golf pros," said Sue Bonthius of Victoria, a five-time Minnetonka CC women's club champion. "That was the social hub of this area. We didn't have all the restaurants and all these places to go to, and people would go there and party. They had a piano bar, they partied, that was their go-to place."

Bonthius, whose family history at the club dates to 1936 and who remembered that she took her first step on the golf grounds at 16 months old while chasing her dad around the course, said the playing grounds were a good fit for her. "I liked the old feeling of it, the old trees," she said. "I just felt comfortable there. I felt comfortable with the people there."

Minnetonka Country Club was more than star-laden, more than friendly, more than old and tree-lined. It was historic.

"Work will be started at once on the Minnetonka Country club's nine-hole course at Manitou," the Minneapolis Tribune reported on March 4, 1917, referring to a wooded area just south of Lake Minnetonka. "The course was arranged by Bendelow."

That would have been Tom Bendelow, the most prolific golf course architect in U.S. history. Bendelow, a native Scot working largely out of Chicago for the A.G. Spalding Co., designed hundreds of U.S. golf courses. A *Minneapolis Morning Tribune* story from 1917 credited him with having designed more than 730 courses in the U.S. and Canada — and his career extended into the 1930s. Bendelow's grandson Stuart Bendelow, whose research resulted in the 2006 book *Thomas "Tom" Bendelow: The Johnny Appleseed of American Golf*, said in a March 2020 conversation with me that he had verified evidence of 560 U.S. courses that Tom Bendelow designed or contributed to. In Minnesota, they included Minikahda, Golden Valley CC, Edina CC, Mankato GC, Winona CC, Northland CC in Duluth, the Lafayette Club in Minnetonka Beach, Detroit CC's Pine to Palm course in Detroit Lakes, Alexandria GC (the second nine of the course Lehman grew up on; he would later become a British Open champion and successful golf course designer) and Interlaken CC in Fairmont. No matter the actual number — and determining such a thing for almost any prolific golf architect is nigh impossible — Bendelow heads the list.

Bendelow never is mentioned among the greatest golf architects of all time, never alongside the likes of Donald Ross or Seth Raynor or C.B. Macdonald. In fact, his design philosophy has been denigrated as "18 stakes on a Sunday afternoon." That is a misplaced potshot. In his book, Stuart Bendelow noted that his grandfather and A.G. Spalding "were not seeking to design and build championship courses or courses to test the honed skills of the best players, but rather courses that new players could enjoy, courses that would improve player proficiency, courses that would

MINNETONKA COUNTRY CLUB

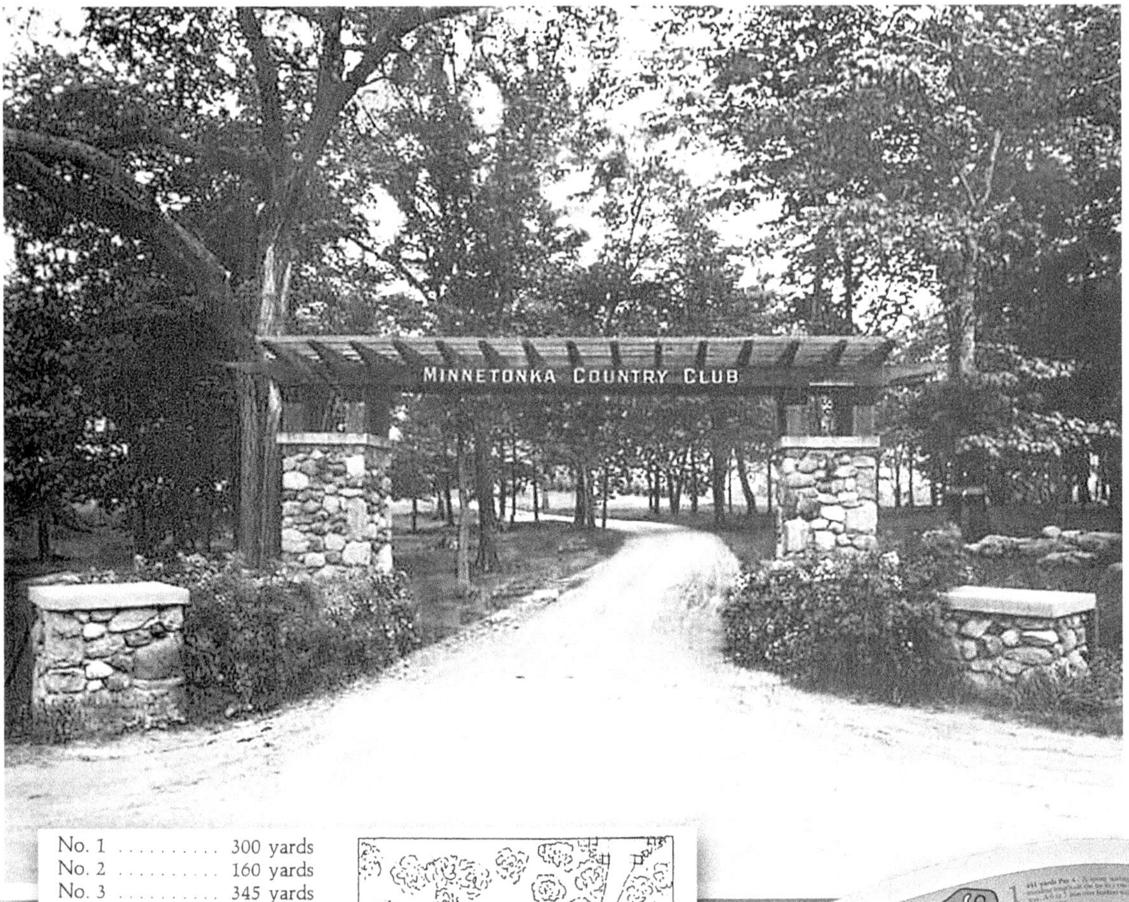

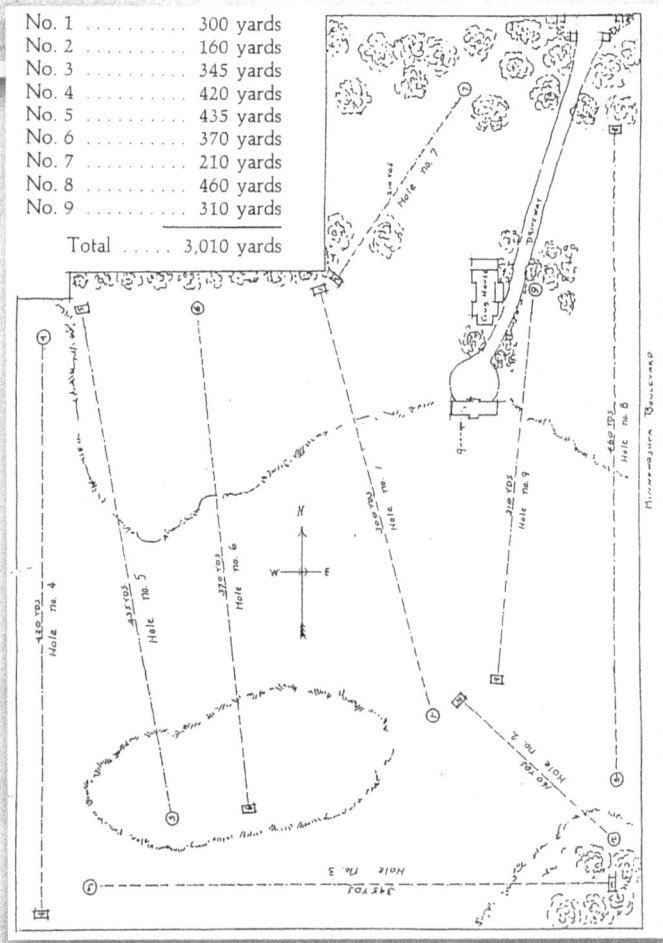

No. 1 .... 300 yards
No. 2 .... 160 yards
No. 3 .... 345 yards
No. 4 .... 420 yards
No. 5 .... 435 yards
No. 6 .... 370 yards
No. 7 .... 210 yards
No. 8 .... 460 yards
No. 9 .... 310 yards
Total ..... 3,010 yards
Hole No. 1
Hole No. 2
Hole No. 3
Hole No. 4
Hole No. 5
Hole No. 6
Hole No. 7
Hole No. 8
Hole No. 9
Club House
Driveway
Minnewashta Boulevard
N
W
E

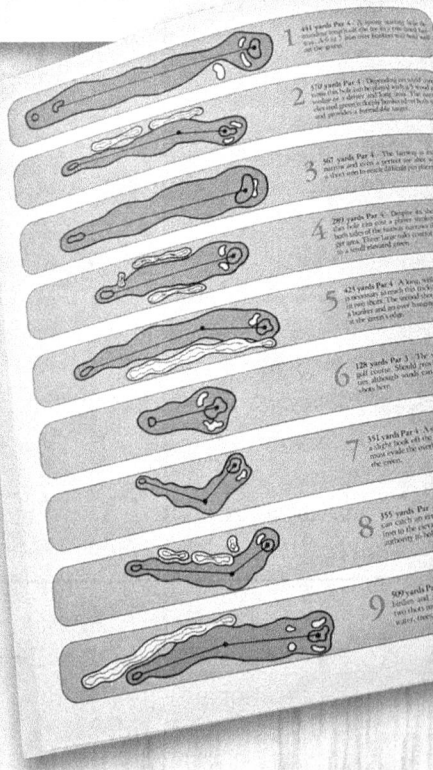

TOP, FAR LEFT: *Entrance to Minnetonka Country Club, 1916. Courtesy of Bob Olds*; BOTTOM FAR LEFT: *Original 1916 layout of Minnetonka CC. Courtesy of Bob Olds*; CENTER: *Hole-by-hole description from 1979 National Car Open program. Courtesy of Bob Olds*; THIS PAGE, CENTER: *Original clubhouse and early description. Courtesy of Bob Olds*; THIS PAGE, TOP LEFT: *Aerial view, Minnetonka Country Club, 1989. In the background is Lake Minnewashta. Twin City Photography, Courtesy of Bob Olds*; THIS PAGE, TOP RIGHT: *On the former site of Minnetonka Country Club, autumn 2019. Joe Bissen photo*; BOTTOM RIGHT: *Along the edge of the former Minnetonka Country Club property, obscured by overgrowth along the side of the road, is an old out-of-bounds stake. Joe Bissen photo*

promote participation, and courses that could be maintained at a reasonable expense." To that end, Tom Bendelow was an American golf success story like no other.

Minnetonka CC has the distinction of having been worked on by both the most prolific golf architect in U.S. history (Bendelow) and the most prolific in Minnesota history (Goldstrand). The latter is credited in many Internet and print entries as having redesigned Minnetonka CC, but Olds' recollection was that both he and Goldstrand, who are friends, redesigned two Minnetonka CC greens each at separate times. Goldstrand, Olds estimated, has designed about 80 courses in Minnesota and the Upper Midwest.

Minnetonka Country Club's life span included many iterations. The club was organized in 1916, and Bendelow laid out the golf grounds that fall on 117 acres in the city of Shorewood. "We have accomplished more than was contemplated," club president Edgar L. Mattson wrote in a January 1917 letter to a prospective member.

"The club house is unique in its architecture," read a 1916 sketch composed by the club, "with wide porches, large dining, living and rest rooms, breakfast room and several fireplaces. The interior is richly finished and panelled throughout with quarter-sawn oak. ...

"The golf course was laid out by Tom Bendelow, of Chicago, and completed under supervision of Robert Taylor, of Minikahda. The land is undulating, permitting links of diversified nature."

The putting greens had grass surfaces and were 80 feet in diameter. The course opened with nine holes at 3,010 yards, with No. 8 the longest at 460 yards and No. 2 the shortest at 160. By 1917, the club had 150 members, the *Minnetonka Record* of Excelsior reported.

From 1917, when the golf grounds opened, until the end, when golf made way for upscale housing development, covering 97 years of history at the club seems tantamount to covering a tee box for the winter with a medium Hefty bag. I can't pretend this accounting will be complete or even hit the high points, but it will feature some details culled from newspapers and from material the Oldses passed along.

- In July 1926, the *Tribune* reported, the club's head pro, Alex Olson, became the first person to break par of 70 on the course, birdieing the final hole for a 1-under 69.

- In July 1928, Jake Wetherby of Minneapolis Golf Club won the club's invitational tournament. The list of entrants included a handful of Minnesota golf greats from that era (yes, I'm name-dropping): Johnston, Bolstad, Sawyer, Rudy Juran, Frank Brokl and Joe Coria.

- A February 1929 note in *10,000 Lakes Amateur Golfer and Outdoor Magazine* detailed changes to the club's 18-hole layout, including significant changes to the front nine, with holes lengthened and holes combined. Among them, the 90-yard "niblick" hole that was the seventh was folded into the eighth, lengthening that hole to 375 yards.

"This 18-hole links combines the unusual qualities of being pleasant to the duffer and intriguing to the expert," the magazine noted.

- A 1932 promotional brochure listed Minnetonka Country Club as 18 holes, greens fees at $1, and "Dance — Cabaret Style."

- The *Tribune* in November 1935 advertised a public liquidation sale for the clubhouse assets — dishes, silverware, carpeting, table and chairs, lockers and more.

- I guess this is history, of some fashion. A blurb from the *Tribune* of Aug. 5, 1940, read: "Em Braak at Minnetonka Golf club reported two whizzers Sunday. Eldon Rothgeb powered a tee shot off the first tee which carried 250 yards, wandered far off line to hit the second tee, and struck a wooden tee lying on the second tee with such force that the tee imbedded itself in Rothgeb's ball. Then up stepped Maury Johnson to the sixth tee and drove his ball into a tree so hard that it bounced back clear over the teeing ground and out of bounds. In spite of this mishap, however, Johnson scored a birdie on the hole, a par five, for he was down in three strokes and, counting the stroke penalty, he had a four."

- An April 1955 story by the *Tribune*'s Bill Carlson announced that the course had been "rehabilitated." The story read in part, "It'll be 18 holes, 6,080 yards, contrasted with the nine-hole layout it has been for the last 12–15 years." The story reported that as World War II approached, "the most accessible nine holes were put together, and the rest of the course abandoned." The new iteration was to be a public course.

- The club was "newly formed" in 1960 as a private club, according to a *Tribune* ad.

- In November 1962, an early-morning fire destroyed much of the clubhouse, with damage estimated at $150,000 to $160,000. An April 1963 photo caption from the *Tribune* indicated the new clubhouse would include a ballroom that would seat 300.

- In 1970, two holes were shortened, four lengthened, and the course went from par 72 to par 70.

- Though the club hosted few significant Minnesota Golf Association events, it did have a run in the 1980s of holding the Women's State Open, also known as the Piper Jaffray Women's Open, and the men's State Open, also known as the National Car Open, in 1979. Winners included Lovander, Kate Hughes and Dan Croonquist.

The historical aspect of Minnetonka Country Club included one feature that was part of the golf course but not related to golf.

A hump.

"When they built the golf course originally," Olds said, "there was a streetcar line that went through the property before the golf course (was built)." It started, Olds said, near Yellowstone Trail, which ran along the southern border of the golf course. The hump of land was about 12 to 15 feet wide, Olds said, and 2 feet high. It went across eight holes on the back nine, including the 14th, on which golfers had to clear the hump.

The streetcar line-turned-hump had presumably connected Shorewood and

More! Gone.

Bob Olds spent 39 years as head professional at Minnetonka Country Club in Shorewood, gathering memories as well as memorabilia.

JOE BISSEN PHOTO

the south-central Lake Minnetonka area with Yellowstone Trail, which was the nation's first coast-to-coast highway. The trail was established in 1912 and ran from Massachusetts to Washington state and through Yellowstone National Park. In Minnesota, it went east to west from Lakeland to the South Dakota border, roughly following the path of what is now U.S. Highway 212.

Olds was an accomplished golfer as well as noted club professional, with one TapeMark Charity Pro-Am championship to his credit. Nancy Olds was a skilled player as well. In their home, the Oldses have a plaque commemorating Nancy's then-course-record 82 at Kingsbarns Golf Club in Ireland — weeks after the historic club had reopened in 2000 after 61 years idle.

Minnetonka CC closed on Dec. 31, 2014, giving way to a still-in-progress residential development called Lennar at Minnetonka Country Club. Some of the new street names are golf-themed: Bentgrass Way, Prestwick Court, Brassie Circle, Featherie Bay.

Bob Olds, who had opportunities to pursue higher-profile positions at notable Minnesota golf clubs, remained true to Minnetonka CC until the end. Nancy Olds said her husband cried the first time they returned to the grounds after the club closed and housing development started. She saluted Bob Olds' loyalty.

"Minnetonka (Country Club) was a family that all became because of him.

The way he treated them was awesome," Nancy Olds said. "Every time I went up there ... there was never any, and not just with us, 'Oh, you're the employee,' it was 'come sit with us.' We got included.

"That prevailed through the whole time we were there and has prevailed to this day, even though the golf course closed. (Club members) are still mourning the fact that they don't have Minnetonka Country Club anymore and how much they miss the whole experience. It was just an awesome place."

Lake Neighbor

Four miles northeast of the old Minnetonka CC site, there is a plot atop a hill, not far from the shore of Carson's Bay, in the city of Deephaven. On that plot once stood the St. Louis Hotel, opened in 1880 by St. Louis attorney Charles Gibson. It was an extravagant place with marble-topped dressers, elegant drapes and large brass beds, according to a story in *Lake Minnetonka* magazine.

It also had a golf course. Maybe. OK, probably.

This item appeared in the *Minneapolis Tribune* of July 1, 1902, and was nearly parroted by an item in the same day's *Minneapolis Journal*.

"A new golf course has been laid out on the hotel grounds under the supervision of N.C. Goforth of St. Paul, who is an enthusiastic golfer, and who, with Mrs. Goforth, has already been several weeks at Hotel St. Louis.

"Daily contests are now in progress in order to make a record for the links, and all the guests are under instruction from Mr. Goforth and Robert Burkam, a Princeton senior."

Despite spending hours trying, I never could confirm that there was a golf course at the hotel, which would have sat only 350 yards from Ward Burton's Minnetonka Ice Yacht Club golf course of the late 1890s and early 1900s. The St. Louis Hotel was torn down in 1907. But the names mentioned in the newspapers strike chords with a few notes I found.

Walter Cyrus Goforth was a St. Paul attorney. His residence, the Goforth House, is listed among St. Paul's historic homes, with an address of 574–576 Lincoln Avenue West. Robert Burkam would have been 20 years old and a student at Princeton University in 1901. He later became a lawyer and a member of Princeton and St. Louis (Mo.) country clubs. And here is the thread that establishes a sporting connection, if only mildly: Burkam's father in law, Horatio Nelson Davis of St. Louis, "took an active interest in athletics and was a devoter to golf," according to an obituary published in 1915.

The thread is strong enough for me to declare, if only tepidly, that there once was a golf course at the St. Louis Hotel.

CHAPTER 8

Pioneering and Vanishing Act

"Never was a golf club formed under more favorable circumstances; never were members more enthusiastic and persevering."

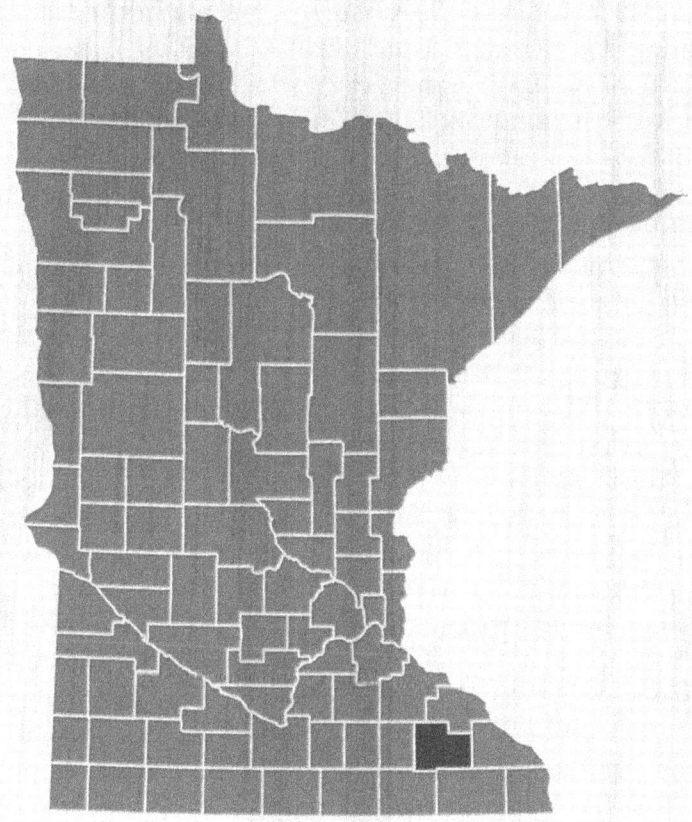

**COURSE: SILVER CREEK GOLF CLUB
CITY: ROCHESTER
COUNTY: OLMSTED
YEARS: 1900-01**

More! Gone.

Minnesota's earliest lost golf courses are long, long gone and mostly long, long forgotten.

But props are in order to a few of the forebearers.

Winona Golf Club was the state's first lost golf course, a sliver of light that flickered for mere months in 1897. WGC led the next year to the establishment of Winona's Meadow-Brook Golf Club, which in 1901 was host of the first Minnesota State Amateur tournament. That course lasted until 1918. Bryn Mawr Golf Club (1898–1910) in western Minneapolis was the Halley's Comet of early lost courses, shining brightly before famously spawning first Minikahda GC in 1899 and then Interlachen CC in 1910 (the same year Bryn Mawr shut down and Halley's made a particularly spectacular celestial appearance). Roadside Golf Club (1897–1902) in St. Paul was Minnesota's first female-friendly early course. Merriam Park (1900–1906) was, like Meadow-Brook and Bryn Mawr, a charter member of the Minnesota Golf Association.

One other seems particularly worth citing.

The first mention of golf that I know of in the southeastern Minnesota city of Rochester was made by the *Rochester Post and Record* of May 11, 1900:

"There is no reason why Rochester should not have a golf club," the newspaper story began, and reported that a group of 12 people had begun efforts to organize one. Membership was to cost "$10 for a gentleman alone or $15 for lady and gentleman together."

By late June 1900, the organization of Rochester's first golf club was imminent. "The game of golf grows greater in popularity with an increasing number of Rochester people," the *Olmsted County Democrat* reported on June 29. "The golf links between the State Hospital and St. John's cemetery have seen more people in the last three weeks than at any other period in known history. ... Golf is a most healthful form of exercise and is much enjoyed by all who have the leisure to play."

A week later, a group of 23 people met at the home of milling company owner John A. Cole and organized the city's first golf club. On July 6, 1900, the *Post and Record* and the *Olmsted County Democrat* both reported on the organization of the first golf club in Rochester.

"The 'Silver Creek Golf Club' is now firmly established in this city," the *Post and Record* reported. "The foundation stone has been laid, and the nucleus is formed from which a flourishing and prosperous club will grow.

"The present links are situated about a mile from the city (remember, this is 1900 Rochester, population 6,843, not the current sprawl of 100,000-plus), just north of the Northwestern railroad tracks, and this side of the State hospital. At present, there are only five holes laid out, but owing to the constantly increasing membership, the club finds it necessary to lay out two or three more holes. ...

"Never was a golf club formed under more favorable circumstances; never were members more enthusiastic and persevering. If this counts for anything, as we know it does, then who can doubt the bright future of 'The Silver Creek Golf club.'"

The club was so named because of its proximity to Silver Creek, which runs from east of Rochester into the city before emptying into the Zumbro River near Silver Lake. The course's grounds are presumed to have lain near what is now 5th Street Northeast and 15th and 17th Avenues Northeast — east of Calvary Cemetery, which went by the name St. John's Cemetery until 1940.

The first set of Silver Creek club officers made for a distinguished foursome in Rochester business and professional society. Cole was the founding president. Arthur F. Kilbourne, the club's vice president, was superintendent of the Rochester State Hospital. Secretary John H. Kahler was a prominent Rochester hotelier; one of the businesses his family started still operates in downtown Rochester as The Kahler Grand Hotel. Treasurer George J. Stevens owned a carpet and window-hanging business.

Though the club's founding members were well-to-do, its golf grounds were modest. "This pasture was maintained by a herd of sheep and a few goats with the greens given more attention by hand mowing," wrote local golf historian James Gardner, the former longtime greens superintendent at Rochester Golf & Country Club, in 1988. It is likely the course "expanded" from five holes to six at some point.

Modesty aside, in its second season of operation, Silver Creek Golf Club

Silver Creek runs quietly through a residential area on the eastern side of Rochester. More than 100 years ago, Silver Creek Golf Club lay on or near this site.

JOE BISSEN PHOTO

helped make Minnesota golf history. On Aug. 29, 1901, representatives of seven golf clubs met in Winona and formed the Minnesota Golf Association. The seven founding clubs were Bryn Mawr and Minikahda of Minneapolis, Town & Country and Merriam Park of St. Paul, Tatepaha of Faribault, Meadow-Brook of Winona and Silver Creek.

Silver Creek was referred to as Rochester Golf Club in Winona newspaper stories documenting the formation of the MGA and as "Rochester Club" in the minutes of the MGA meeting. But as sure as Jordan Spieth can putt, the Rochester club that was a founding MGA member had its grounds on the Silver Creek site. The club is referred to as Silver Creek in a *St. Paul Globe* story of Aug. 30, 1901, that reported on the formation of the MGA, and the newspaper reported that "Cole" — presumably John A. Cole — was elected an MGA director. The *Minneapolis Tribune* also referred to the club as Silver Creek. The minutes of the MGA meeting list "Ireland and Terry" as delegates of "Rochester Club" — and H.J. (Harry) Terry and W.W. Ireland also were listed as Silver Creek members in Rochester newspaper stories from 1900.

And then, poof. Almost as soon as Silver Creek Golf Course came onto the scene, it disappeared.

Or didn't. Take your pick.

Advancing past 1901, I could not find firm evidence that Silver Creek Golf Club saw the dawn of 1902. An archivist's search at the Olmsted County Historical Society revealed no mention of Silver Creek golf from 1902–15. I contacted three authors, including Gardner, who had mentioned Silver Creek in writing about the origins of Rochester Golf & Country Club, and none could confirm that the course existed during that 1902–15 "dead period." One Minneapolis newspaper reference to a Rochester club in 1903 is as easily debunked as verified.

The years 1915–17 marked a pivotal period in the development of Rochester golf. There are slightly different versions of stories afoot, but the essence is that Rochester Golf Club was formed, and play began on the club's current site two miles west of downtown, known today as Rochester Golf & Country Club. Harry Turpie, professional at Red Wing Country Club, designed the original nine holes at the current site, and famed architect A.W. Tillinghast produced an expansion to 18 holes in the late 1920s. Today, RG&CC is one of Minnesota's preeminent courses, having hosted the MGA State Amateur Championship five times.

And what of the Rochesterians who in 1900 pumped drives into Silver Creek or fanned mid-mashies into the cemetery? Those people were not one-year golf wonders. As with other golfers at early Minnesota lost courses, many took up the game at new venues, and some became promoters and pioneers of the game.

Gardner confirmed that Silver Creek members Kilbourne, Ireland and Terry also were early Rochester Golf & Country Club members. Harold J. Richardson, a University of Minnesota law student in 1900 who "suffered a 'swipe' in the face with a golf stick" at Silver Creek, according to the *Olmsted County Democrat*, recovered to become a prominent attorney, moved to St. Paul, and had memberships at Town & Country Club, Minikahda, Somerset and White Bear Yacht Club. Certainly, there were other Silver Creek members whose games emigrated to other courses.

And so, Silver Creek joins a group of Minnesota lost golf courses that are gone but should not be forgotten.

More information on early golf in Rochester is in a version of this chapter at ForeGoneGolf.com.

CHAPTER 9

Common Threads

*"I remember (sand greens)
were horrible to golf on.
... It's like putting in a sand trap."*

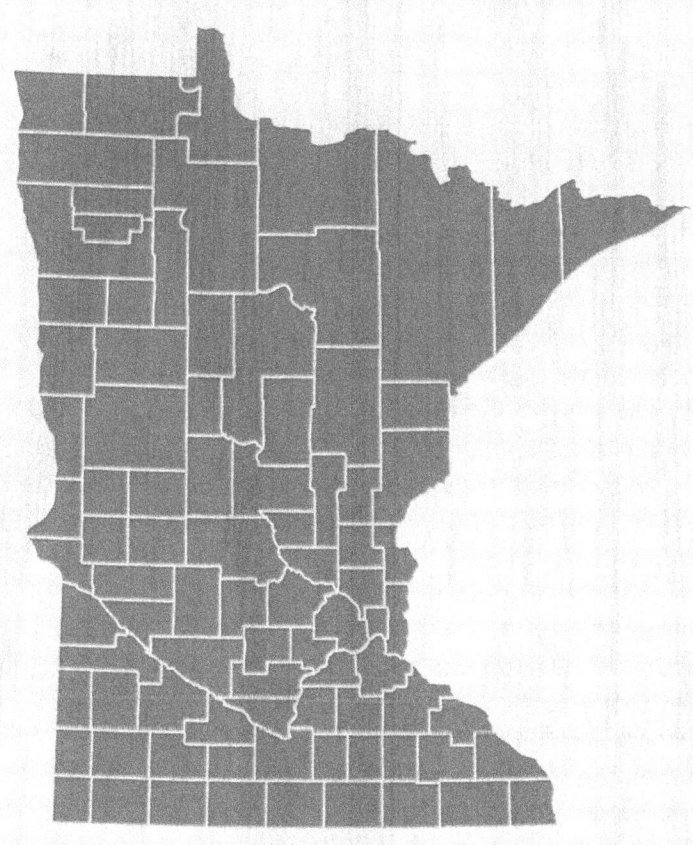

More! Gone.

WHERE THERE ARE LOST GOLF COURSES, THERE ARE ...
Lost golf course sites.
Lost photographs.
Lost scorecards, lost scrapbooks and lost memories.
And, sadly, lost golfers.

Little tangible evidence remains from most of Minnesota's lost golf courses, especially from those abandoned before 1950. The people who played them are mostly gone, too. The precious few remaining men and women who remember the lost courses of the 1930s and '40s are almost all 90 or older.

Reconstruction of these courses, then, is a challenge. Did they all look the same? Did they have common characteristics? If we're trying to compare an old, lost course to a modern, existing one, how do we do that?

Those answers are "no," "yes" and "it ain't easy, but think small."

First, of course the lost courses didn't all look alike. This is Minnesota, after all, not high-plains West Texas. They were built on prairie flatland (as at Marshall, for instance) and on hillsides (Riverdale) and near terrain that rolls and folds like the bedding you just climbed out of (Lake City). They were built next to bodies of water (Princeton Golf Club, Cass Lake Golf Club) and on high urban ground (Lakeview/Hillcrest).

But there are common threads, too. Remember that most of these courses were built in the 1920s, a decade not only of quantity in golf construction but quality as well. The '20s, in fact, are referred to as "The Golden Age" of golf course design.

Nationally, architects such as Donald Ross, A.W. Tillinghast and Seth Raynor were designing world-class layouts in the 1920s. All three plied their craft in Minnesota at one time or another. Regionally, the prolific Tom Vardon, who also served as head professional at White Bear Yacht Club, and the even more prolific Tom Bendelow of Chicago, who is credited with more than 550 U.S. designs, were among those who laid out notable courses in Minnesota — although Bendelow's work in Minnesota came almost exclusively before 1920.

It would be laughably presumptuous to think that every man who designed a 1920s Minnesota golf course was a disciple of Ross or Raynor or "Tilly," but there were distinctive characteristics among many of the state's 1920s courses. Notwithstanding the farmer or banker who strolled into an empty field, blithely planted nine flagsticks in the ground and declared his golf course open for bad-bounce business, they tended to look like this:

"It was very much a matter of fitting the golf hole to the land," said Chaska golf course architect Kevin Norby in 2014, "as opposed to today, where we just go out there and take the land and scrape away and do whatever we want to do."

Tom Fazio, a golf course architect known worldwide, said much the same in his book *Golf Course Designs*:

A sand green on the lost Chisago Golf Course, 1920–circa 1943. As with most sand greens, not what you'd consider long on architectural inspiration.

COURTESY OF CHISAGO CITY HERITAGE ASSOCIATION.

"Many of the things done by Donald Ross or A.W. Tillinghast or William Flynn were dictated by the limitations of machinery and construction methods," Fazio wrote. "Their design decisions might fairly be described as 'rub of the green,' rather than rub of the designer's pen, because they didn't have the equipment to do otherwise. Nature made the decision for them."

In a word — a word used by Norby — the design philosophy was "minimalist."

Island greens and amphitheater mounding were a half-century off. Early course architects rarely had more than a couple of teams of horses drawing plows with which to carve the landscape, if they had any desire to carve the landscape in the first place.

Still, pure minimalism was not a good option on green sites. Any designer worth a five-dollar retainer's fee would recommend at least some moving of the earth for the benefit of the short game.

Norby cited Keller, the estimable public course in Maplewood which opened in 1929 and was laid out by Paul N. Coates, a Ramsey County engineer who received golf course design advice from Ross, as a case study of early-1900s courses.

"You go to a classic golf course," Norby said, "and the greens are elevated, round and small. They were built with a horse and buggy, and they were put on top of hills.

"Keller's a really good example. You look at the backs of greens, and those little bumps are areas where the dirt was pushed off to make the green." (Keller underwent a significant revamp, overseen by Richard Mandell, that reopened for play in 2014.)

Norby said greens on classic courses tend to be flatter and smaller than present-day greens -- approximately 3,000 to 4,500 square feet, compared with some of the behemoths of today, which can reach 11,000 square feet.

Greens construction on classic courses was relatively simple, Norby said. Manure, sand and topsoil were mixed to create putting surfaces.

Often, the formula was less complex than that. A lot of sand, a little oil, and voila, there's your green — your sand green. If ever a golf term belonged in the Oxymoron Hall of Fame, "sand green" would be it.

Many of Minnesota's early golf courses featured sand greens. The "design" concept was simple: Dig out a circular target area, fill it with sand, apply some form of oil — crank-case was said to be the most effective — to keep the sand in place and the texture constant, and provide a special two-sided rake, one side with a toothed edge and the other side with a smooth edge.

Yes, golfers did (and still do, in very rare cases) actually putt on sand greens. When a group completes play on a hole, the "green" surface is to be raked or swept to make it as smooth as possible for the next group. Protocol, as explained in 2013 on the website pasturegolf.com, is as follows:

"Task of sweeping the greens usually falls to the loser of the hole."

Sand greens could be positively — or negatively, one might say — microscopic. An April 26, 1934, *Mower County News* story on the construction of the lost Hillcrest Golf Course in Austin reported that the course was to feature "sand greens that are approximately forty feet in diameter."

The concept of having to putt on these tiny beasts was attractive to few golfers.

"They were hard to putt," said Irous Nelson, 94, of New Richmond, Wis., who recalled playing a sand-greens course in the Windom, Minn., area. "In the first place, on the old courses, they weren't taken care of."

An even less-ringing endorsement came from Dave Palmquist of Winona, who played the lost sand-greens course at Whitewater State Park near St. Charles.

"I remember they were horrible to golf on," Palmquist said. "They're not nearly as predictable as the greens today, that's for sure. It's like putting in a sand trap. Nothing rolls very predictably. I never was a good golfer, but I struggled a lot on those sand greens."

Sand greens, however, often were the only reasonable option for a fledgling course with limited funds for construction or upkeep. They were cheaper to maintain than grass greens. Special mowers were of course unnecessary, as were aeration, herbicides and pest control -– well, unless there was concern about the extremely remote possibility of a desert iguana setting up camp on a Minnesota sand green.

One other thing about lost courses of the early 20th century: They were economy-sized, at least in relation to those of today. Golf in those days was played with hickory-shafted clubs (steel shafts were introduced in 1925) and non-high-tech-gizmoed balls. A smite of 250 yards qualified as mighty in those days. Courses, in turn, had to fit the game as it was played then — no 7,000-yard titans allowed.

A version of this chapter appeared in Fore! Gone.

CHAPTER 10

Back Home on the Farm

"I learned to play golf using the backside of my dad's left-handed putter."

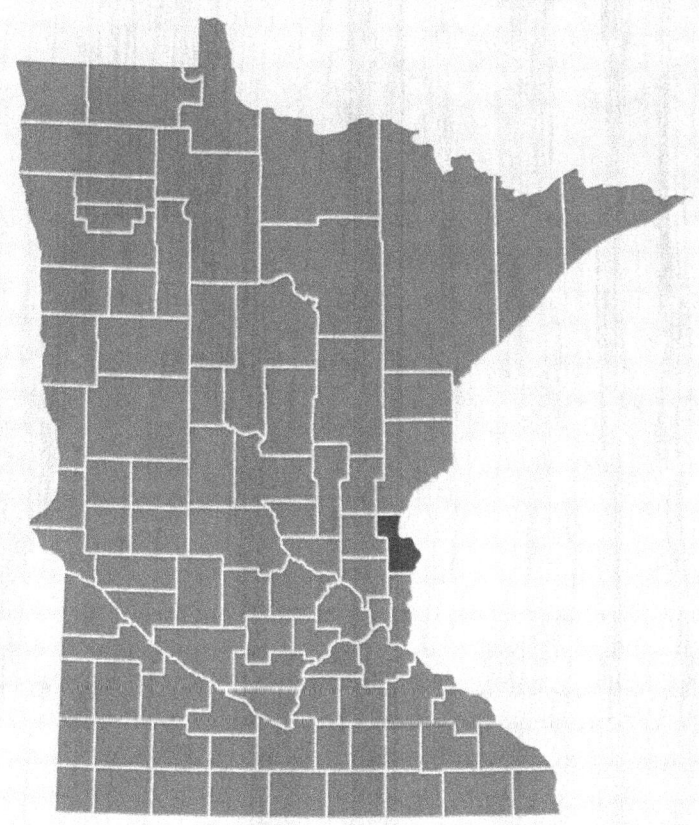

**COURSE: RUSH CITY COUNTRY CLUB
CITY: RUSH CITY
COUNTY: CHISAGO
YEARS: 1934-54**

More! Gone.

July 2015

RUSH CITY, MINN. — "WELL, SHOULD WE TAKE A LOOK?"

Don Johnson had popped the question.

Don Johnson, on the site of the former Rush City Country Club. Much of the golf course land is in the background.

JOE BISSEN PHOTO

Johnson and I were spending a late afternoon exploring. We had driven into northern Chisago County and pulled off the road. We were starting at an open field when he up and said the six magic words:

"Well, should we take a look?"

Um, yeah, Don. We should take a look. I mean, after all, it's a lost golf course. Why wouldn't we take a look? Why wouldn't anyone?

Oh, plenty of reasons, not that any of them were going to stop us.

Such as:

Bumps and brambles. This was rolling turf, overgrown with grass, weeds and thistles, shin-high to knee-high. It wouldn't be an expedition up the sheer face of El Capitan, but it wouldn't be a walk in the park, either. Tumble-and-fall potential: maybe 10 percent.

Also: The temperature was 90. Humidity was up there, too.

And: Johnson was 87. As in years of age.

"Eighty-seven and a half," he had gently corrected me a bit earlier.

Not to mention: Carl Heinrich's advice.

OK, I just mentioned it.

A month earlier, Heinrich, who owns property just east of where Johnson and I were standing, had suggested in a phone conversation that exploring the premises, especially the wooded area surrounding nearby Rush Creek, might not be prudent. Something concerning large, hairy animals with sharp incisors and powerful forepaws.

Not that I cared. Not that decency prevailed, either, which would have prompted me to suggest, say, this rejoinder to Johnson:

"Sure, Don, let's go look around, but just FYI, I've been told there might be bears close by, perhaps eager to consume our major organs and leave the rest of our rotting entrails over by the second green."

No, I shut up. I wanted to explore the 60-year-old resting place of Rush City Country Club as much as Johnson did.

We forged ahead.

"The Rush City Golf Course was developed in 1932–33 by Arthur 'Art' and William 'Bill' Johnson on the J.P. Johnson farm east of Rush City," reads the first sentence in *Rush City Golf Course*, a detailed, illustrated booklet written by Art Johnson's son Don — the same Don Johnson who was exploring the abandoned course with me.

This image, scanned from Don Johnson's "Rush City Golf Course" booklet, shows the first hole at Rush City Country Club, circa 1940. The hole was a 135-yard par 3, crossing Rush Creek. The sand green is visible to the left of two smaller trees toward the top-left of the photo.

JOHNSON TOOK THE PHOTO AFTER CLIMBING THE WINDMILL ON THE FAMILY FARM.

"The design and construction of the golf course," the booklet continues, "was assisted by Pete Carlson, who developed and operated the golf course on Sand Lake near Moose Lake MN. The (Rush City) course was first opened for play in 1934."

To be more specific, Rush City Country Club (or Golf Course, or Golf Club; it was referred to all three ways) was situated one mile east of downtown Rush City, off Chisago County Highway 55. Across the road to the north in modern times lies a farm field and then the southern edge of Rush City Regional Airport. The golf course lay just south of the highway. Bisecting it during its playing days was Rush Creek, a serpentine stream that ultimately empties into the St. Croix River.

If anyone knows the lay of the land, Johnson does. He grew up on the property, slept and ate and studied in the home that also served as the golf clubhouse. He played Rush City CC as a youth and helped the family manage the farm and golf course before graduating from Rush City High as the class salutatorian in 1945. He attended the University of Minnesota and went on to work in the Twin Cities as a mechanical engineer for Honeywell.

Johnson, who is retired and now lives in Lindstrom, later developed an interest in his Chisago County and western Wisconsin roots, became a genealogy expert and history buff, and wrote the *Rush City Golf Course* booklet a decade ago.

A few more passages:

"The golf course was first developed by tiling and draining land along Rush Creek, which was already beginning to dry up in the early 1930s. The course of Rush Creek was altered to fill and straighten one of the horseshoe bends. Three holes followed the course of the creek. As originally designed and built, the golf course was a par 36. The greens were oiled sand, as were most of the country courses at that time.

"Frequent stories in the Rush City Post tell of various golf tournaments being held, pitting the locals against teams from Braham, Cambridge and North Branch starting in 1934.

"... As the ground along Rush Creek became wetter near the end of the 1930s, the golf course had to be altered and shortened two different times until it became only a par 29. Thereafter, only two holes, #1 and #7, crossed the creek, and none played along Rush Creek.

"During the winter of 1934–35," the booklet continued, "the clubhouse was remodeled and in the spring of 1935 was opened for dances several nights a week in addition to golf. ... From 1935 until about 1943 Saturday night dances were held at the club house with beer, set-ups and hamburgers being sold. A 5¢ slot machine was also operated in the club house but was always moved out of sight into the ladies rest room when notification was received that the sheriff was coming for a visit.

" ... The golf course continued to operate until about 1954, although never regaining the popularity and tournaments of the 1930s and early 1940s after the end of WWII."

Johnson's newspaper clippings featured ads: "Herman Sandquist and his orchestra will play at the club" ... "Hamm's and Glueck's Beer on draught" ... "Shot-gun Turkey Shoot ... Use your own gun and ammunition."

Johnson and I tromped into the field. We approached the only standing building in sight — although "standing" hardly seems the operative word. An old granary, tilted so badly you'd swear you could knock it over with a properly placed whisper, leaned out toward the golf grounds, standing sentry, as it did 75 years earlier, near the corner of what was a dogleg on the first hole of the course's original design.

That opening hole would be replaced in Rush City CC's later, wetter years by a par 3 of 135 yards that crossed Rush Creek. The hole today would be considered the antithesis of a proper golf hole — instead of a grass green with a sand bunker beyond, it had a sand green with a grass bunker beyond.

Old No. 1 was memorable for Johnson. "There was a kid, I was in first grade and he was in second grade," Johnson told me a couple of weeks earlier in a phone conversation. "We played the first hole, and he beat me. He got the first hole in 12 shots, and I did it in 13.

"The thing is, we went on and went to school together and played sports together, and I never could beat him at anything."

You could blame the equipment, Don, and no one would think the worse of you.

"I learned to play golf using the backside of my dad's left-handed putter," Johnson said.

Moving on, we came upon old concrete blocks yards south of the granary. They were part of the foundation of Johnson's childhood home — in other words, the old Rush City CC clubhouse. Almost nothing remains of the building. A patch of day lilies planted by two of Johnson's aunts in the mid-1930s still blooms alongside the foundation. The two-story house was burned down in about 1990, Johnson said, in order to ensure a clear path for craft flying in and out of the nearby airport.

Though Johnson is the preeminent authority on Rush City Country Club, then and now, Heinrich offered a couple of recollections as well.

"When I bought that land," Heinrich said, "I found so many golf balls. I gave a 10-pound sack of them to some kid as payment for working for me."

Also, he recalled, "I had this hired hand; he'd see golfers go out and chop at the grass. If we had boiled eggs for breakfast, he'd put them out there, and the golfers, they'd go out swinging away and looking for the balls — and they'd be eggshells."

Johnson and I saw a good share of the old Rush City Country Club grounds that warm summer day, and he later e-mailed me with a second batch of information that included his memories of how the course was tended, that it likely closed in about 1954, and he passed along aerial photos with overlays of the course's routing. All can be viewed at ForeGoneGolf.com.

I can also thankfully report that we were not eaten by bears.

CHAPTER 11

Minneapolis Mystery

*"It plays over a beautiful course
of nine holes laid out in the
Camden park region
and crosses the creek three times."*

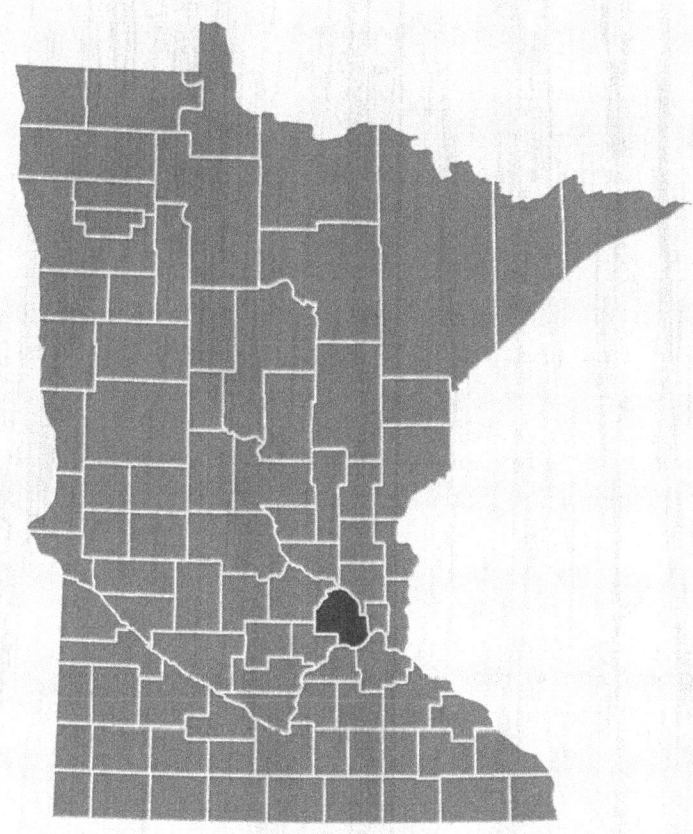

**COURSE: CAMDEN PARK GOLF CLUB
CITY: MINNEAPOLIS
COUNTY: HENNEPIN
YEARS: 1899–CIRCA 1905**

More! Gone.

IN LATE AUGUST 2014, WHILE WALKING THE TRAILS ALONGSIDE THE MISSISSIPPI RIVER IN NORTH MISSISSIPPI REGIONAL PARK, I CAME UPON THE MOUTH OF SHINGLE CREEK, THE POINT AT WHICH IT EMPTIES INTO THE RIVER. REMEMBERING THAT I HAD WRITTEN ABOUT THIS APPROXIMATE LOCATION IN FORE! GONE., WITH A FOUR-PARAGRAPH PASSAGE ON AN ALMOST–UNKNOWN COURSE CALLED CAMDEN PARK GOLF CLUB, I GOT AN ITCH TO WRITE ABOUT LOST GOLF COURSES AGAIN.

Infernal itch. Looks like I'll try to figure out where Camden Park GC is buried.

Camden Park Golf Club? The north Minneapolis locals, even those with deep knowledge of the area's history, were mostly skeptical. "You know anything about the golf course that used to be around here?" (I mean, it was only a century ago.) That was met with quizzical, doubting looks. You'd think I had asked, "You know anything about the Yeti colony that used to live around here?"

Yes, there was a Camden Park Golf Club in north Minneapolis, in the Camden neighborhood and near the intersection of Lyndale Avenue North and what is now Webber Parkway. Almost no one has heard about it because the club was obscure and short-lived.

Six documents — the only ones I know of that mention Camden Park Golf Course — confirm its existence:

- From the July 21, 1899, *Minneapolis Tribune*, by way of the blog of Minneapolis Parks historian David C. Smith: "The Camden Park golf club has been organized among the young men in the employ of the C. A. Smith Lumber company." The new club, the *Tribune* reported, had a membership of 25 and growing. "It plays over a beautiful course of nine holes laid out in the Camden park region and crosses the creek three times." Smith presumed (correctly) that the reference was to Shingle Creek.

- The 1899 *Harper's Golf Guide*, passed along by Joe Gladke, includes a Camden Park entry. The guide said the club was organized in 1899, listed membership as 25, and listed the club officers, including President G.T. Forest and a rarity, a woman on the advisory board: Miss Nannie Smith. Gladke also passed along a newspaper story that listed the names of the nine holes: Nemo, Ann, Anon, Tacit, Willows, Woods, Creek, Baby, Home. The greens were reported to be "natural," which presumably meant they had grass surfaces, not sand.

- This, from the national 1901 *Harper's Golf Guide*: "CAMDEN PARK GOLF CLUB - Post-office address, Camden Place, and sub-station, Minneapolis."

- An almost-identical entry appears in the 1902 *Official Golf Guide* published by The Grafton Press of New York.

- The golf club is mentioned in a 1905 Minneapolis city directory, with a

Shingle Creek spillway, near the eastern edge of Webber Park. This feature was built in 1980, long after Camden Park Golf Club closed.

JOE BISSEN PHOTO

listed address of "Camden Park Place Athletic Club, 4157 Washn Ave N."

I had speculated in *Fore! Gone.* that the course might have been within a few hundred yards of the Mississippi River, near the current I-94 corridor and the Camden Bridge.

Mea culpa. Sorta. I think I was wrong. After spending parts of three months revisiting the subject — walking the area, talking with local residents and experts, googling up a storm, and viewing old plat maps and city directories — I believe I can say this, firmly and unequivocally, about the site of Camden Park Golf Club:

Heck if I know exactly where it was.

Two theories remain in play for me. A third seems less plausible. Here are the cases for each theory, using 42nd Avenue and Lyndale Avenue North as a base point:

To the east

Theory: Camden Park Golf Club was east of Lyndale Avenue, occupying what is now part of the I-94 corridor and the southern edge of the North Mississippi Regional Park grounds.

Likelihood: 10 percent.

Why it could have been: The course was, after all, named Camden Park, and this is the plot that would have been closest to Camden Park — the original Camden Park. At the time Camden Park GC was organized, Camden Park was east of Lyndale Avenue and 42nd Avenue North, not far from the Mississippi River. A new Camden Park was established in 1908, west of Lyndale. That park now goes by the name Webber Park, so renamed in 1939.

The reference in the *Harper's Guide* to "sub-station" as part of the location could have been to the Shingle Creek Pumping Station, which essentially abutted the river on ground that now is a parking lot and launch area at the south end of North Mississippi Regional Park.

Also, considering that the course was organized and/or played by employees of the C.A. Smith company, whose massive lumber mill was based at 4400 Lyndale Avenue North, it's possible the golfing enthusiasts used part of the lumber mill land for their fledgling course.

Why it probably wasn't: Not enough room. On this plot, the place would have been nicknamed Claustrophobia Country Club. Though the Camden Park course was short by today's standards, totaling 1,586 yards and with a longest hole of 235 yards, there almost certainly would have been too much neighborly interference to have accommodated even nine short holes here.

To the west

Theory: The Camden Park Golf Club grounds occupied an area that is now mostly the eastern edge of Webber Park. Golf-course borders would have been just north of what is now Webber Parkway, extending possibly as far north as 44th Avenue North, and possibly almost as far west as Dupont Avenue. To put it in modern terms, think of the area around the Shingle Creek spillway, the Bridge of Dreams and where the Webber Park swimming pool is, and you have the likely resting grounds of Camden Park Golf Course.

Likelihood: 80 percent.

Why it could have been: Many reasons. 1) Three Shingle Creek crossings, as referenced in the 1899 *Tribune* story, would have been eminently feasible (incidentally, Shingle Creek in 1900

The eastern edge of Webber Park, at Webber Parkway and Lyndale Avenue, and likely former grounds of Camden Park Golf Club.

JOE BISSEN PHOTO

nearly abutted what is now Webber Parkway; it was later re-routed about 100 yards to the north, up against the railroad tracks). 2) The "sub-station" reference can be explained by the possibility that it might have been to the nearby post office outlet and not the pumping house. 3) The area would have been larger than the relative broom closet east of Lyndale.

Camden golfers might have been afforded a nearby check-in station at this site — call it a clubhouse if you wish. The 1901 *Harper's Guide* lists club officers, including "Chairman of House Committee, W. H. Trabert, 4247 Washington Avenue, North Minneapolis." That address, now 4247 Webber Parkway, is directly across the street from the current Webber Park. Trabert lived at the same address as one Charles L. Trabert, president of the Camden Park Golf Club and a clerk at the C.A. Smith Lumber Company (the 1906 *Hudson's Directory of Minneapolis* says so). I'm thinking the Traberts might have checked in folks at their house, sent them on their way across the front yard and Washington Avenue, and onto the greensward.

Why it might not have been: No good reason I can think of. But I can't exclude other grounds as long-shot possibilities, so I'm not going to unequivocally state that the old Camden Park Golf Club grounds is on the site of the current Webber Park. Still, my reasonably educated guess says it is.

To the north

I'm leaving open a remote possibility the golf course was in an even larger area north of 44th Avenue North and west of Dupont Avenue — but that site was so far removed from Camden Place and Washington Avenue that it seems unlikely.

Likelihood: 10 percent.

More about Camden Park Golf Club:

- Members of the club probably were not the types who pushed and pulled on C.A. Smith's crosscut saws for 11 hours, then brushed the sawdust off their flannel shirts and walked over in their work boots for a leisurely nine holes. The club officers were white-collar: Vice president Chester Ellsworth was a lawyer in the Loan & Trust Building, secretary J.O. Wells was a dentist who appears to have boarded with the Traberts on Washington Avenue, and treasurer Carl G. Krook was a lawyer in the New York Life Building (my, that surname was unfortunate).

- Here is the full text of the 1901 *Harper's Guide* entry:

CAMDEN PARK GOLF CLUB.— Post-office address, Camden Place, and sub-station, Minneapolis. Entrance fee: $15. Annual dues, $1. Membership, 35. A nine-hole course. Distances and bogey figures: 1, 135, 6; 2. 140, 4; 3. 218, 5; 4. 235, 6; 5. 196, 6; 6. 110, 3; 7. 162, 4; 8. 200, 4; 9. 190, 5. President, Charles L. Trabert; Vice-President, Chester Ellsworth; Secretary, Dr. J. O. Wells, Camden Place, Minneapolis; Chairman of House Committee, W. J. Trabert, 4247 Washington Avenue, North Minneapolis; Treasurer, Carl G. Krook. Greenkeeper: Herbert J. Anderson.

CHAPTER 12

Fun and Games

"… (These were) humble folks with day jobs."

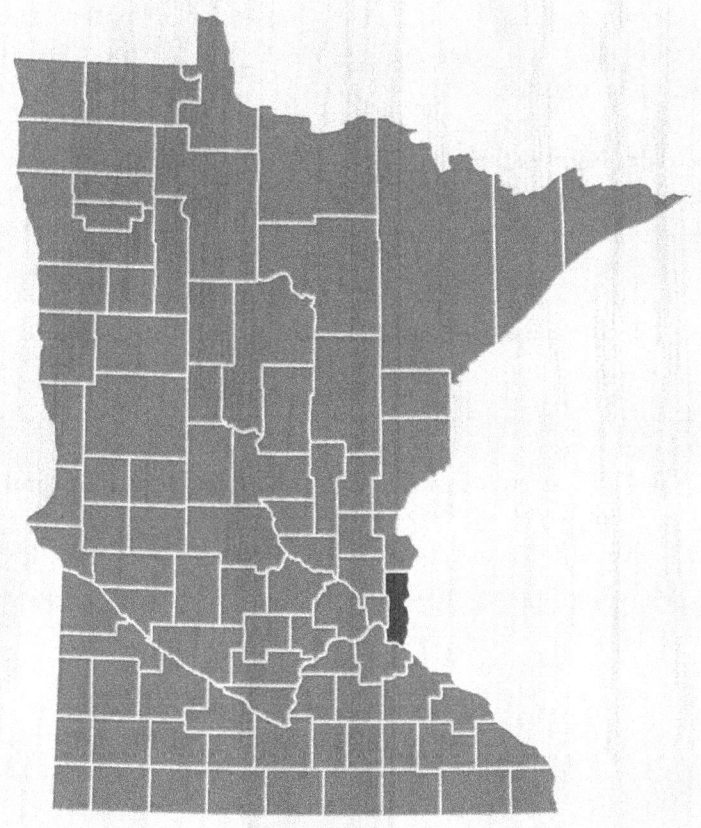

COURSE: CASTLE GREENS COUNTRY CLUB
CITY: OAKDALE
COUNTY: WASHINGTON
YEARS: 1960–82

More! Gone.

"It was kind of like the corner bar — out a ways."

OAKDALE WAS A DIFFERENT PLACE IN THE 1960S. NOT DIFFERENT AS IN ODD OR UNUSUAL. DIFFERENT AS IN NOT THE SAME AS IT IS TODAY.

Today, Oakdale, an eastern suburb of St. Paul, is a city of 28,000. Think freeways, strip malls and more cul-de-sacs than Minnesota has lakes, or at least it seems like it.

In 1960, by contrast, Oakdale didn't even exist as a city. The northern half of what is now Oakdale, known then as Northdale, was mostly undeveloped, with all the suburban sprawl of, let's say, Chugwater, Wyoming (real place).

So yes, "out a ways," as John Elert put it, is a fair assessment in 1960s terms.

About that corner bar, otherwise known as Castle Greens Country Club: It featured more than beer and Seagram's. And most folks who frequented the place thought of it as North St. Paul, not so much Oakdale.

"The first tee was right there," Elert said in September 2019, standing a couple of hundred feet off Century Avenue in northern Oakdale and pointing to a spot just behind Silver Lake United Methodist Church. "There was a huge putting green. There was a pond right in front of the first green. ..."

"Two was up a big hill, about a hundred yards or 90," continued Elert, then proceeding with an abridged version of Castle Greens' entire nine-hole routing, including the trailer court just beyond the golf course's eastern edge. It's still there, named Twenty-Nine Pines.

The lie of the land was different then. That big hill is gone. So is the one that was on the ninth hole, about 30 feet high, Elert estimated. All of the hills are gone, razed and flattened for housing development after Castle Greens closed.

Memories, however, remain.

"I remember walking behind a tractor and picking up rocks and (helping turn) a farm field into (a golf course) and how labor intensive this was," said John Elert's brother Jim, whose father, Dick, was a co-founder of Castle Greens. Jim said he was under 10 years old at the time. "They took a barn and made a two-story golf club and supper club, with what kind of money?"

In an e-mail, Jim called the founders "humble folks with day jobs."

The barn originally belonged to Fred Boessel, Jim Elert said, and stood next to his cornfield. It was converted into the Castle Greens clubhouse for the country club's debut in the summer of 1960 — pro shop and golf equipment downstairs, plus recreation, dining and dancing upstairs with a long balcony attached. The building now houses the Methodist church, with services observed on the second floor.

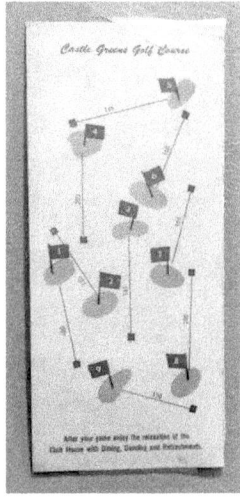

COURTESY OF JIM ELERT

Partly because Oakdale wasn't incorporated as a city until 1968, Castle Greens long had more of a North St. Paul identity than an Oakdale one. The three founders — Dick Elert, Hal Norgard and Bob Engwer — were noted North St. Paul figures. A fourth key figure, greenskeeper Ron Belland, who along with the founders helped build the course from scratch, was mentioned in a November 1963 Minnesota golf superintendents' newsletter as being from "Castle Greens C. Club, No. St. Paul." (Belland's uncle Jack Belland helped build Keller Golf Course in Maplewood.) Geographically, the designation made sense, as North St. Paul lay just across Minnesota 120 (Century Avenue) from Castle Greens' clubhouse.

That North St. Paul identity really never went way, Jim Elert wrote in the e-mail. "Up until the day the course closed, golf shirts, caps, scorecards, and advertisements always indicated North St. Paul as the location."

Even the club's name whispered "North St. Paul." Castle Greens, Jim Elert said, was dubbed as such by his mother, Connie, in a name-that-club contest. She had known the city of North St. Paul was originally named Castle, in honor of Henry Anson Castle, a prominent city journalist, politician and businessman in the late 1800s.

Yet one thing the club didn't whisper, despite its name, was the preconceived notion of "country club." Though membership was private at the start, one doesn't usually think of a par–3 course, such as Castle Greens, as a country club. Holes ranged in length from 102 to 230 yards, and some of Castle Greens' ancil-

Castle Greens Country Club co-founder Dick Elert, left, with his son Jim, behind the counter at the clubhouse.

COURTESY OF JIM ELERT

Mary Elert, daughter of Castle Greens co-founder Dick Elert, at the course in August 1965 at age 8.
COURTESY OF JIM ELERT

lary activities would decidedly not be considered country clubbish.

Not the miniature course immediately north of the clubhouse. Not the trapshooting range just north of that. (There was a driving range between the two.) And not some of the side ventures: snowmobile sales and rental, Christmas tree sales.

Castle Greens was, however, a social club as much as it was a golf club. Wedding receptions and New Year's parties were held there, with hundreds of guests, Jim Elert said. A 1968 *Minneapolis Tribune* story advanced a luncheon "for Miss America" that would be held there as part of North St. Paul's Snow Frolics celebration. In 1982, Castle Greens helped host "the largest ever St. Paul Winter Carnival Softball Tournament on ice," the *Minneapolis Star* reported, with more than 5,000 participating on Silver Lake, just across Century Avenue in North St. Paul.

"I think for this little part of town," Jim Elert said, meaning North St. Paul, "it was its own little golden age of social and whatever. You wouldn't have to be a golfer because of all the different evening things and the parties that the spouses (could go to)."

On the course, Jim Elert recalled night golf, with participants wearing lighted miner's-style helmets and playing with fluorescent balls. He recalled that four golfers shared the course record of 3-under-par 24, and the surnames will look familiar: brothers Don Elert, Marv Elert and Dick Elert, as well as Gib Runnels.

Among the Elert brothers' favorite memories were the end-of-season racehorse tournaments. Champions from 10 leagues at the club would tee off together on the first hole. One golfer would be eliminated per hole, with beverage-toting spectators wagering trinkets (heavens, not real U.S. currency, oh no that would never happen) on which golfer would advance. "By the time you get to the ninth tee," Jim Elert said, "there were two people, and one person wins and the partying commences."

The golfing and festivities continued through the 1982 season, when Castle Greens Country Club closed and housing development started. Trapshooting continued into the 1990s. A swamp that lay north and east of the golf course site was filled, presumably with earth taken from the former golf course, and used to create a par–3 course named Oakdale Greens, later named Oakdale Par 3. That course was abandoned in 2009, and today that land lies undeveloped.

John Elert, left, and his brother Jim, sons of Castle Greens co-founder Dick Elert, on the former grounds in September 2019. They are standing on the current grounds of Silver Lake United Methodist Church, which formerly served as the Castle Greens clubhouse. The golf grounds was primarily to the right (east) of where the Elerts are standing.

JOE BISSEN PHOTO

CHAPTER 13

Picture This

*"Edge of town. Altitude 1,117 feet. ...
Green fee to be moderate."*

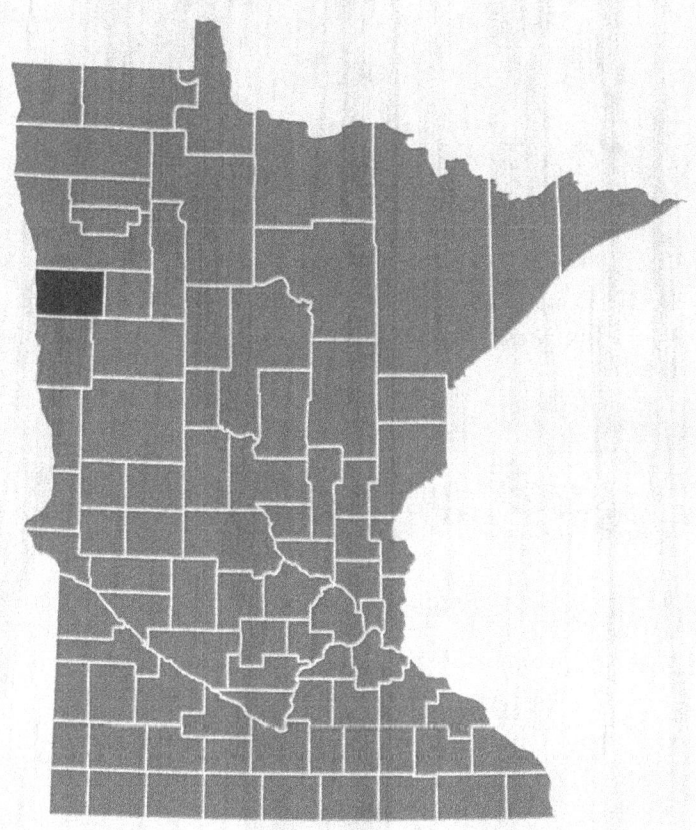

COURSE: TWIN VALLEY GOLF CLUB
CITY: TWIN VALLEY
COUNTY: NORMAN
YEARS: 1926–CIRCA 1930

More! Gone.

A CHAPTER IN "FORE! GONE." INCLUDED A ONE-PARAGRAPH ENTRY ON TWIN VALLEY GOLF CLUB IN NORTHWESTERN MINNESOTA, TAKEN FROM A NORTHERN PACIFIC RAILWAY GOLF DIRECTORY. IT INCLUDED THESE PRECISE AND HELPFUL NOTATIONS (THAT'S SARCASM): "EDGE OF TOWN. ALTITUDE 1,117 FEET. ... GREEN FEE TO BE MODERATE."

Altitude?

In 2019, I happened across an undated postcard of the course, prompting a search for more information. I found just a little. I place my research efforts ahead of the railway directory editor but behind those of, say, Barbara W. Tuchman in her *A Distant Mirror: The Calamitous 14th Century*, 677 riveting I'm sure pages.

Twin Valley Golf Club was organized on April 21, 1926, according to a report in the *Twin Valley Times*, with T.L. Croswell as president. The Croswell family was noted for building power plants in northern Minnesota, including one at Heiberg, an unincorporated town one mile north of Twin Valley, and the *Times* story said the course was laid out "near the Croswell Power Company's plant at Heiberg."

A 1939 aerial photograph, presumably taken after the golf course had been abandoned, shows two old green sites just east of Highway 32, near the Wild Rice River and Mashaug Creek. Indications from the aerial photo are that the northern edge of the golf course might have been as far north as alongside Highway 200.

The club counted 22 members at its time of founding, with membership set at $1.00 plus "20 hours of labor, or its equivalent." The last mentions I found of Twin Valley Golf Club were from 1930 — first a match at Fertile in which B.L. Howard was medalist with an 82, then a rematch two days later played "in a sandstorm" at Twin Valley.

Another highlight, of sorts? The *Twin Valley Times* of April 6, 1927, heralded the approaching golf season by noting, "The green's (sic) committee ... are not at present planning the destruction of a number of gophers."

My word-count checker says this chapter is 344 words. Your call as to whether this picture is worth 344 words.

CHAPTER 14

Famed Flight, Not-So-Famed Golf Course

"There is no better tonic than a chase after the little white ball before breakfast."

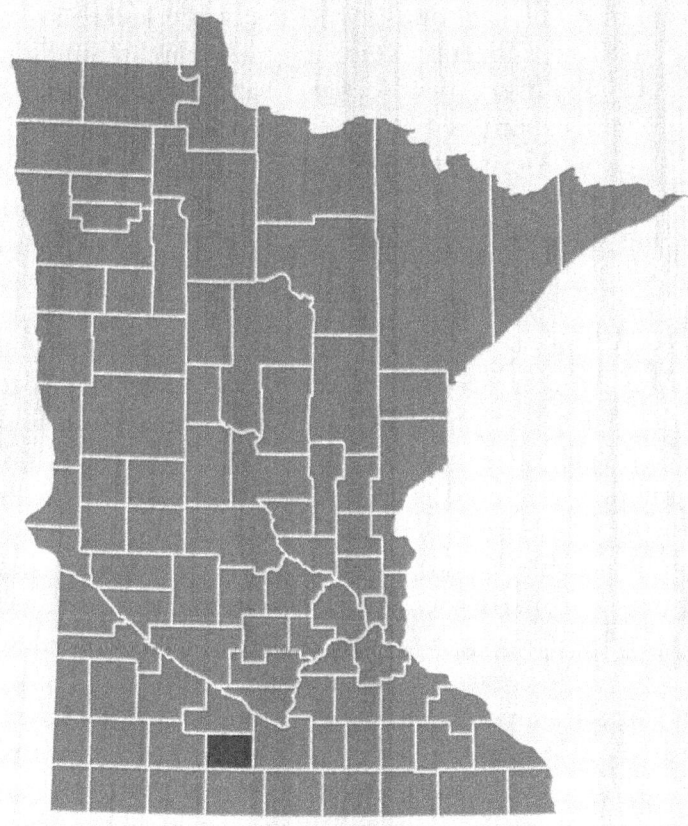

COURSE: MADELIA GOLF CLUB
CITY: MADELIA
COUNTY: WATONWAN
YEARS: 1921–CIRCA 1930

More! Gone.

Moments in southwestern Minnesota history:

Sept. 21, 1876, west of the city of Madelia, along the banks of the Watonwan River: Shots fired.

May 1921, west of the city of Madelia, not far from the banks of the Watonwan River: Shots fired again.

Honestly, one shouldn't make much of the similarities. They are coincidence, nothing more. The "shots" couldn't have been more dissimilar. And although the first incident stands as perhaps the most significant event in Watonwan County history, the second, by comparison, is about as historically significant as Rory McIlroy clipping his fingernails next Wednesday.

Dispensing with the historically significant first:

In September 1876, three members of the James-Younger gang, which had been foiled 14 days earlier in an attempt to rob the First National Bank of Northfield, made their way through Madelia and then westward as they fled justice through the small towns of southern Minnesota. On Sept. 21, three of the Younger brothers — Cole, Bob and Jim — plus fellow gang member Charlie Pitts skulked through an area known as Hanska Slough until making a last stand in the Watonwan River, just south of the town of La Salle. A gunfight ensued. Pitts was shot and killed, and the Youngers were captured.

The Northfield bank robbery is considered one of the most famous in U.S. history. The Youngers' attempted escape has been retold in book, magazine and even poetry form and has been the subject of preservation and re-enactment.

As for the second shots-fired event, only a handful of souls around Madelia know anything about it. Stacked up against the story of the Youngers, may we present a few dozen paragraphs of sheer anticlimax:

Forty-four and a half years after and 5.5 miles east of the site of the Youngers' capture, different brands of foursomes, less threatening than three Youngers and a Pitts, made their way to an area west of Madelia, a few hundred yards north of the Watonwan riverbank.

The *Madelia Times-Messenger* of May 27, 1921, explains:

"The Madelia Golf Club is now a reality," the newspaper reported, "a sufficient number having signed the membership roll to make a go of it.

"At a meeting held Monday night, Dr. R.J. Hodapp was made temporary chairman and Dr. M.J. James acted as temporary secretary. It was decided to place the membership fee at $5.00 for this season, and each membership to include the immediate family of the person joining the club.

"A portion of the Siron pasture, comprising about 25 acres, has been secured for the course, and those who are acquainted with the game claim that this tract will make as fine a golf course as is to be found anywhere. It will be a nine-hole course, and there are a sufficient number of mental and physical hazards to satisfy the most exacting."

A mural on the Chamber of Commerce building in downtown Madelia depicts the capture of the Younger brothers near La Salle.

COURTESY CITY OF MADELIA CHAMBER OF COMMERCE

" ... It is expected that grounds will be ready for play on Memorial Day."

In reality, Madelia Golf Club probably belied the "best course anywhere" boast.

The course was established on an attractive piece of land straddling Elm Creek, two miles west and slightly north of downtown. But its features were rudimentary, in a golfing sense. A *Times-Messenger* story from May 6, 1921, foreshadowed as much:

"Golf seems to be generally considered a rich man's game, but we are told that such is not necessarily the case," the newspaper reported. "Elaborate grounds, club houses, banquets, etc., are not at all necessary. Any old pasture of fifteen or twenty acres will do for a nine-hole course, and its use will not in any way interfere with the cattle which are pastured upon it."

Bessie, here we come, mashies in hand.

The Madelia course, laid out by four members of the club's grounds committee, was maintained by livestock grazing on the Siron pasture, which actually was part of the Fred Tiedeken farm, according to Barb Nelson of the Watonwan Historical Society. Although most Minnesota small-town courses of the 1920s and '30s featured sand greens, which offered at least a modicum of refinement in rolling a ball across the land, the Madelia course had natural-grass greens, albeit probably less than Augusta-smooth. And golfers occasionally had the distinct displeasure of having to rinse their cowpie-tainted golf balls in nearby Elm Creek, according to Adeline Yates, whose father, Buster Yates, grew up nearby and wrote about the course in his 1986 book, *Seventy-Five Years on the Watonwan*.

"When the course was next to our place," Buster Yates wrote, "my neighbor buddy, Lucius Siron, and I caddied for the players at a dime a round of nine holes. In our spare time we hunted lost balls and sold them back to people. During hard rains the balls would wash down the hills into the creek from where we would pull 'em out with a garden rake. The old creek produced more than golf balls; in the spring of the year bullheads, northern and walleyed pike and others headed north out of the river for Wilson Lake spawn. (Wilson Lake lies 1.5 miles to the north.)

"During these years the golfers didn't have the benefit of daylight saving time for afternoon golfing and a clubhouse for celebrating afterward. Consequently, the course was buzzing with activity at daylight on summer days. Merchants played a round before opening their shops for the day.

"The golf club hired George Lassak, night operator at the railroad depot for part time service in keeping the greens in shape. The grass on the rest of the course was clipped short by our band of a hundred sheep. George didn't have more than fifty dollars' worth of tools. A hand push lawn mower, a few rakes and shovels, plus free help from our sheep kept a well-groomed golf links."

Madelia Golf Club's inaugural season appears to have been a success. On Oct. 21, 1921, the *Times-Messenger* filed this note: "These beautiful October mornings find many of our golf enthusiasts on the links bright and early. There is no better tonic than a chase after the little white ball before breakfast."

On March 20, 1922, Madelia Golf Club drew up articles of incorporation. In late June 1922, the club announced it would be staging a tournament — single-elimination, match play, with handicap — to run through the Fourth of July. And a piece of potentially big news came later that summer. Doc Hall made the announcement with a piece written for the Aug. 18 edition of the *Times-Messenger*:

"William Clark, professional of the Oak Ridge Country Club of Minneapolis, and a nationally known golf course architect, laid out the nine-hole course of the Madelia Golf Club, Wednesday. He was assisted by several of the members who volunteered their services for the day.

"Mr. Clark was somewhat puzzled by the topography of the land but finally succeeded in laying out what promises to be an extremely 'sporty' golf course.

"The total length of the nine holes will be approximately 2880 yards, the shortest hole being 125 yards in length and the longest 550 yards. The creek and sand pits and several hills are used to good advantage in providing the necessary hazards. Mr. Clark remarked on first seeing the course that the land was peculiarly adapted to golf purposes. Only two holes, the third and ninth, will be trapped.

" ... After he was through someone asked Mr. Clark how the Madelia course would compare with other courses elsewhere in the state. He replied, saying, that outside of some in the Twin Cities, the local course would surpass anything that he knew of in the state. He said that the old course was only 'cow pasture pool' but that now it could be classed as a real golf course.

"Completing his work here, Mr. Clark returned to Minneapolis on the 5:01 train and promises to send the necessary blue prints and instructions for the building up of the course. As soon as these are received the officials of the club will endeavor to start as soon as possible on the construction of the course."

It was a brush with greatness, or at least prettydarngoodness. Clark was indeed a noted golf course architect. He designed or contributed to the design of at least a dozen Minnesota layouts, including Oak Ridge in Hopkins; Minnesota Valley in Bloomington; Northfield Golf Club; Superior (now Brookview) in Golden Valley; Minneapolis municipal courses Columbia, Armour (now Gross), Southwest (now Meadowbrook) and Glenwood Park (now Wirth), and a lost course in Chisago City.

Clark's plans for Madelia Golf Club never came to pass. The historical society's Nelson, in conducting extensive research of the *Times-Messenger*, found no evidence that the club ever made the improvements Clark suggested. By October 1922, the club was in financial distress and seeking an assessment of $10 per member to improve the grounds, a request gussied up by a social gathering and dinner that included "fried chicken ... potatoes in various styles, fruit salads, rolls, jelly, apple and pumpkin pie, cheese and coffee," the newspaper reported.

I'll be right over with a 10 spot, if it's not too late.

Beyond that, references to Madelia Golf Club are scant. Nelson wrote in an email: "The 1923 newspaper has only two short notices about a golf tournament and scores from that tournament. The 1924 had no information on the course. In August of 1925 Joe Jansen was recognized as Madelia's champion golfer, after he made the course in 38."

Madelia Golf Club likely lasted only until about 1930. That is the approximate closing date posited by Yates in his book.

CHAPTER 15

Mr. President, Here's What You Missed

"Coolidge played out of obligation and his game reflected it, as he usually required double-digit shots on each hole."

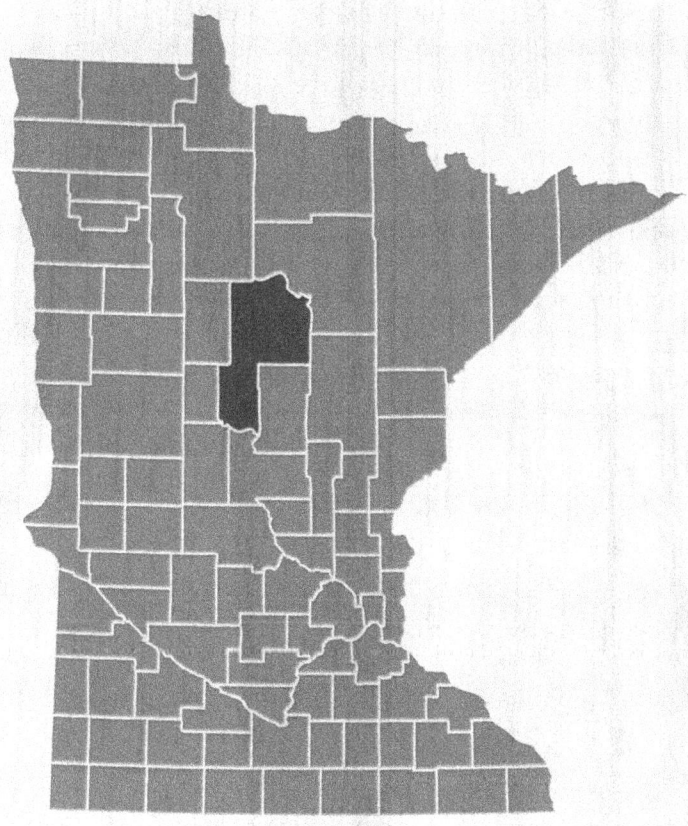

COURSE: CASS LAKE GOLF CLUB
CITY: CASS LAKE
COUNTY: CASS
YEARS: 1926–38

More! Gone.

T**he story of golf in the northern Minnesota city of Cass Lake does not start with an attempt to lure the U.S. president to town.**

But a story has to start somewhere, so this is it ...

On March 11, 1927, Henry George Bingham of St. Paul composed a letter, typewritten on paper carrying the letterhead of the St. Paul office of the Mutual Benefit Life Insurance Company, to M.N. Koll, secretary of the Cass Lake Commercial Club. Bingham, who owned a resort lodge on the western shore of Cass Lake, informed Koll that he had heard President Calvin Coolidge had been invited to spend his summer vacation in northern Minnesota — at the Woodhome Lodge, an hour southeast of Cass Lake on Roosevelt Lake near the city of Outing.

Bingham thought Cass Lake — and The Bingham, as his lodge was known — would be a superior presidential destination. He told Koll so in his letter and implored him to write to Coolidge, inviting him to Cass Lake for the summer.

The next day, Koll composed a letter that would soon be eastbound. Today, a copy of it rests in the archives of the Minnesota History Center. The letter began:

"Subject — Summer White House.

"My dear President:

"The late Edmund L. Pennington, had a summer home here for several years. He was the Chairman of the Board of Directors of the Minneapolis Saint Paul and Sault Ste. Marie Railway when he died about a year ago. It was sold to Mr. H.G. Bingham shortly afterwards by Mr. Pennington's Estate.

"It is modern. It has very choice equipment. It is half a mile from the village limits. Has telephone, electric lights, $5,000.00 cabin launch suitable for the waters of the lake system here. Has an east frontage, fine bathing beach, stands on a bluff overlooking the lake facing the famous Star Island. Has equipment to care for over thirty guests. Has both separate lodges and sleeping rooms in the main building. Has a golf links adjacent. It is quiet. It is situated among the pines."

Koll listed more Cass Lake organizations and assets and proclaimed that "we can lay claim to a high average of intellectuality in the community." The sum total of the letter was to invite Coolidge

Calvin Coolidge, sans Grace and Betty

to spend part of his summer at The Bingham.

Off the letter went to Washington, D.C.

Koll received acknowledgement of the letter's arrival in correspondence dated March 15 and written on White House stationery. The White House's reply was noncommittal.

But ultimately, no dice. On May 31, the White House formally announced, to great fanfare from Midwestern newspapers of the day, that Coolidge and his travel contingent — including his wife, Grace, and her pet porcupine, Betty — would spend their summer at Custer State Park in the Black Hills of South Dakota.

Cass Lake's loss, Black Hills' gain. Henry Bingham, Mathias N. Koll and Cass Lake Golf Club went on about their 1927 daily routines, sans the Coolidges and their prickly pet rodent.

In a sporting sense, perhaps it's just as well. Silent Cal might not have enjoyed himself at Cass Lake Golf Club. "Coolidge played out of obligation and his game reflected it," *Golf Advisor* reported in a 2014 story, "as he usually required double-digit shots on each hole."

Cass Lake Golf Club's nine-hole, sand-greens course had not yet begun its second season when Bingham and Koll composed their letters. The club was organized in 1925 and opened play on and near Bingham's property in 1926.

"It has long been the desire of the people of Cass Lake Village," read a *Cass Lake Times* article in July 1925, "to add to its many other attractions — golf grounds."

A committee of 10 businessmen was formed to search for such grounds. A.C. Anderson of Hibbing, Minn., described as "a golf expert," was invited to visit Cass Lake and offer opinions on a suitable tract. The decision was made by the newly formed Cass Lake Amusements Inc. to employ land on the "Sam Fairbanks Allotment," as the *Times* put it, "or that part of this allotment that lies between the 'Boat Landing Road' the Soo Line railway and Cass Lake."

"This is a beautiful ground, rolling, covered with a vigorous second growth of timber, and having a splendid outlook upon Cass Lake, the several islands, the Minnesota National Forest and practically all of Pike Bay."

Eat your heart out, Cal. And Betty.

Cass Lake Golf Club's prehistory began with four holes that lay on the Bingham Lodge property before the club was organized. After the club organized on June 28, 1926, five more holes were built after the acquisition of

Bingham Lodge promotional brochure, 1937

adjacent land on what the *Times* referred to as "the Newsome property."

If all of this is leading to the notion that Henry Bingham was the father of golf in Cass Lake, I'll just say I don't think that's true. I never found a connection between Bingham and the game of golf. But his predecessor on the lodge property, Pennington, well, that's a different story.

Edmund Pennington was born in 1848 to an English father and Scottish mother. He rose through the railway ranks to become Soo Line president. In 1910, Pennington County in northwestern Minnesota was named for him. Pennington lived in Minneapolis' prestigious Lowry Hill neighborhood, and his name is linked in published biographies with names such as Pillsbury and Bovey, both residents of Wayzata's well-to-do Ferndale neighborhood. (Charles Bovey was a founder of Woodhill Country Club in 1915, and much of the Ferndale populace was connected to early Minnesota golf.)

I would bet a stringer of plump Cass Lake walleye that Pennington built four golf holes on his northern Minnesota estate before his death, after which Bingham became the land owner.

Summertime entries in the *Cass Lake Times* of 1926 tell of Cass Lake Golf Club's preparations in building a course. On Sept. 2, 1926, the newspaper reported, "The first casualty on the Cass Lake Golf Links occurred last week, while Mr. and Mrs. C.W. Hough were playing. Mrs. Hough swung on the ball, (Cyril says it was the prettiest shot she has made this year) and Cyril admiring the shot didn't move fast enough and the ball hit him in the eye, laying his cheek open."

The exact whereabouts of Cass Lake Golf Club has proved difficult to determine. I'll spare the details, though some are on my website, ForeGoneGolf.com. The *Times* story from 1925 identified the site as between the "Boat Landing Road," the Soo Line railway and the city proper. That would be the northeastern part of town, possibly within the current city limits or possibly just outside.

Cass Lake Golf Club operated on this site into the 1930s. In 1933, memberships cost $15 and greens fees were 50 cents. The club had an organizational meeting in April 1938, the *Cass Lake Times* reported, and an inter-club match was played against Bemidji in May 1938.

In 1939, Cass Lake Golf Club moved across town, to a site one mile southwest of downtown. It operates there today as Sandtrap Golf Course.

In 1945, Henry Bingham sold his lodge to fellow St. Paul resident Davidson Burns, who renamed it The Burns. Carl and Freda Bixenstine bought the resort in 1952 and operated it until 1969. It operates today under the name Cass Lake Lodge.

Henry George Bingham, who worked at the Curtis and St. Paul hotels after selling his lodge, died in 1948. Seems a safe bet that he never met Calvin Coolidge nor witnessed what surely was the considerable hitch in his golf swing.

CHAPTER 16
St. Paul's "Lake" Mysteries

"On April 6 work was started on the first ten holes of their new course ... and on April 10, players used the course for the first time."

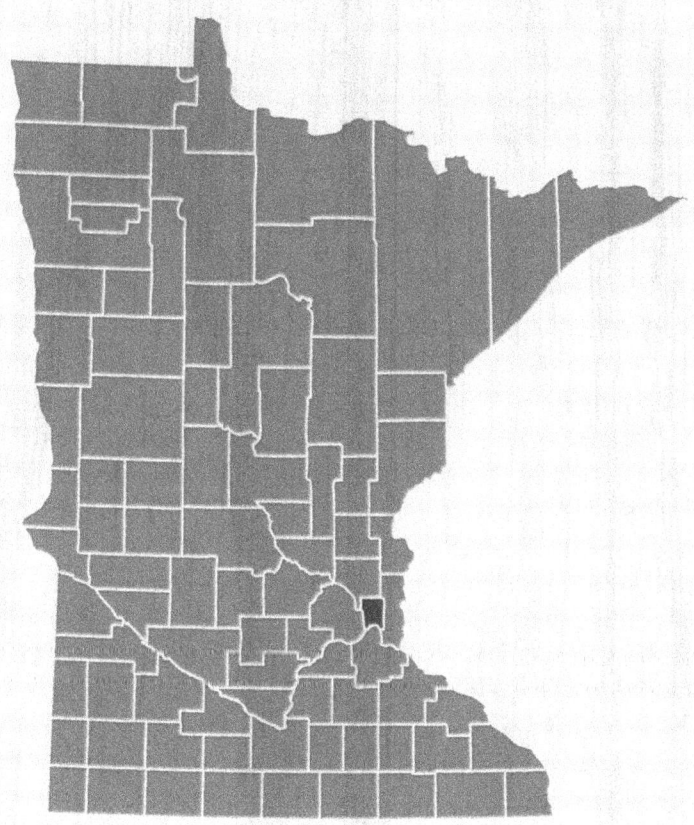

COURSES: READ THE CHAPTER TITLE, ABOVE.
THEY'RE MYSTERIES. WAIT FOR IT.
CITY: ST. PAUL
COUNTY: RAMSEY
YEARS: 1921–LATER THAN THAT

More! Gone.

APRIL 2019

Presenting a Minnesota golf mystery. See if you can figure this out faster than I did. Only took me two years.

Spoiler alert: I'll be giving away the answer a few paragraphs hence. I guess that'll take the "mystery" out of play, but whatever.

Check out, from the Minnesota Golf Association's archived membership rolls, this list of "St. Paul" golf clubs from 1921:

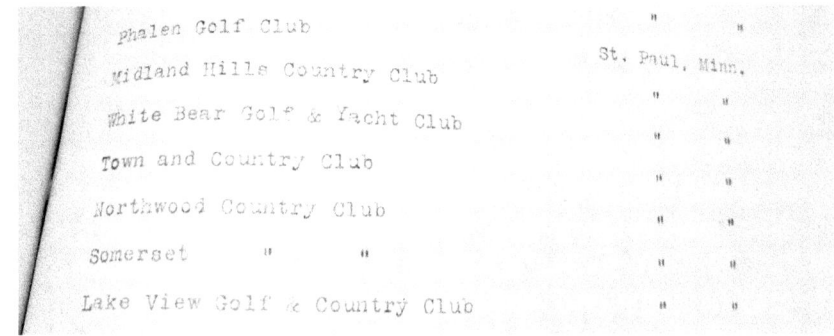

MINNESOTA GOLF ASSOCIATION ARCHIVES

Refrain from geographical nitpicking, please, and scroll down to the final entry. (I'll do the nitpicking — Midland Hills is in Roseville, White Bear Yacht Club is in Dellwood, Northwood was in North St. Paul, Somerset is in Mendota Heights. Something tells me the MGA didn't feel the need to be geographically precise in those days, and that's fine.)

OK, final entry in the photo:

Lake View Golf & Country Club (ditto marks indicating St. Paul).

Lake View Golf & Country Club? In St. Paul?

Never heard of it. What lake, what view, what golf, what country club? It was a mystery to me when in 2017 I was offered a look at the MGA archives and noticed the entry.

Care to take a stab at it?

There aren't a ton of lakeside areas in or very near St. Paul, so some possibilities are easily eliminated. Lake View couldn't have been tied to Phalen Park; that club was established in 1917 and is listed in the MGA membership roll referenced above. Lake View wasn't tied to Como; that golf club's course opened in 1930.

So … Lake View?

Twitter lent an unwitting hand in solving the mystery when in 2019 a golf historian tweeted to me this photo, taken from a page in the 1922 *American Annual Golf Guide*:

ST. PAUL—LAKEVIEW GOLF & COUNTRY CLUB.
Holes—9. Length—3,000 yds. Grass greens. Pres., F. H. Romer; Sec., P. R. Johnson, 514 Guardian Life Building; Chmn. Greens Com., Jas. H. Muir; Professional, Carl Lindgren. Reached by street cars. No limit to number of visitors. Visitors' charges—$1.00 per day. Sunday play permitted and caddies available.

This was presumably the same club as Lake View in the MGA membership roll. Lake View (or Lakeview) Golf & Country Club, found!

Well, sort of. Except there really was no "where" there in the golf-guide entry. With my curiosity again piqued, I was off to the Minnesota History Center in search of Lakeview Golf & Country Club's still-mysterious location. I struck gold — my gold standard is a low one — on one of the first microfiched sports sections I spooled up.

From the St. *Paul Sunday Pioneer Press* of May 1, 1921, this headline:

"NEW GOLF COURSE WILL OPEN TODAY"

"The Lakeview Golf & Country Club will entertain golfers of St. Paul today," the story began. "... The Lakeview Club was organized by enthusiasts of the great Scottish pastime, who for the past two or three years have played on the Phalen municipal course. When the course became overcrowded, certain of its patrons decided to organize the Lakeview Club.

"An excellent strip of land in the northeast end of the city was purchased this spring and work on the first nine holes was started immediately. It is expected that before the close of the playing season that the limit of 200 members will have been ..." (paragraph cuts off)

The rest of the article described the course's rolling terrain, elevated vantage points and various holes. Accompanying the story was a large map of the grounds and routing. At the perimeters were the giveaways. The course was bordered by Larpenteur Avenue on the north and Winthrop and East avenues on the west and east, respectively (East Avenue is now McKnight Road).

St. Paulites and many Minnesota golfers will recognize the description. Lakeview Golf & Country Club was what came to be known as Hillcrest.

The history of Hillcrest Golf Club is well-documented. It was best known as the east metro's Jewish golf club for more than a half-century, although those Jewish roots were first established

at nearby Northwood Country Club in North St. Paul, which opened in 1915. Northwood was abandoned in the 1940s, and some of its Jewish members soon purchased Hillcrest, which was a public course at the time. Hillcrest was sold to a local pipefitters union in 2011 and abandoned in 2017. Its grounds are now vacant.

But the genesis of Hillcrest — or Lakeview, at the start — is less well known. There are no club documents from its earliest years, I've been told. There is little available information otherwise: the aforementioned 1921 article, plus one in a *Minneapolis Tribune* story from the same year suggesting the new Lakeview club was private. But it isn't impossible to cobble together a short history of Hillcrest-when-it-was-Lakeview.

The *Pioneer Press* of April 24, 1921, touted the impending start of the golf season. The headline: "St. Paul to Have Two New Golf Clubs Equaling Best in the West." The first of these was University Golf Club, which soon would be renamed Midland Hills and, through the talents of famed golf architect Seth Raynor (identified as "Rayner" and "Raymore" in the *Pioneer Press* story), would indeed become a regionally prominent golf club.

The second club mentioned was Lakeview, and though as Hillcrest it also would become a golf course of distinction, it is unlikely, considering its staggering pace-of-construction timeline, that it began as one.

"Lakeview golfers believe they have set a record in course construction," a note at the end of the April 14 story reads. "On April 6 work was started on the first ten holes of their new course in Hayden Heights, and on April 10, players used the course for the first time. The record seems a remarkable one. The remaining eight holes will be constructed soon."

I never did figure out under whose breakneck-paced guidance the routing, stump pulling, grading, fairway canting, bunkering and greens swaling of Lakeview was engineered in just five days (yes, that's gentle sarcasm). However, those who have played Hillcrest will note that the routing shown in the 1921 *Pioneer Press* map is different from what they played, and it apparently took only months for the membership to ponder a redesign of Five-Day Lakeview.

"Lakeview club golfers are planning to make an 18-hole course of their links," read the opening of a story in the July 31, 1921, *Pioneer Press*. "... Tom Vardon, White Bear professional, will be in charge of operations which will get under way at the earliest possible moment."

Vardon, who was the head professional at White Bear Yacht Club and designer of more than 40 Upper Midwest courses, is cited in almost all credible references as the original designer of Hillcrest Golf Club. It would be needless nitpicking to challenge that, so I won't. "Mr. Vardon was impressed with the turf covering the tract and declared that it is of a variety that takes years to develop," the *Pioneer Press* story continued. "The second nine holes will be constructed on land that has been under cultivation for years and must be plowed and seeded."

The bulk of the Vardon re-routing of Lakeview lasted for decades, albeit with revisions under the direction of A.W. Tillinghast in 1936–37. The club's name didn't last nearly as long.

The *Pioneer Press* referred to the club as Lakeview for the rest of 1921 and in tournaments in April and May of 1922. On May 14, 1922, the newspaper reported that the clubhouse would be moved closer to Larpenteur Avenue at the club's northern edge.

More references to Lakeview are found in July and August of 1922 and early April 1923, but on April 22, 1923, a *Pioneer Press* story mentioned a new watering system that had been installed at "Hillcrest," and from that point, the club was listed as Hillcrest whenever I found a printed mention. I found no information on reasons behind the name change.

Which brings up another question: What lake gave Lakeview its name?

The reference most likely was to Beaver Lake, one mile south of the Lakeview/Hillcrest grounds. However, none of the Hillcrest-connected folks I talked with said Hillcrest offered a view of Beaver Lake, though most conceded that there might have been such a view in the course's less-densely wooded 1920s.

St. Paul resident Ross Walkowiak, who is well-versed in Minnesota golf history and far more adept technologically than I am, put together a graphic piece that should be of interest to anyone who was familiar with the routing of Hillcrest Golf Club.

St. Paul Short-timer

A second St. Paul lost course that originated in the 1920s is mentioned in the 1923 *American Annual Golf Guide*:

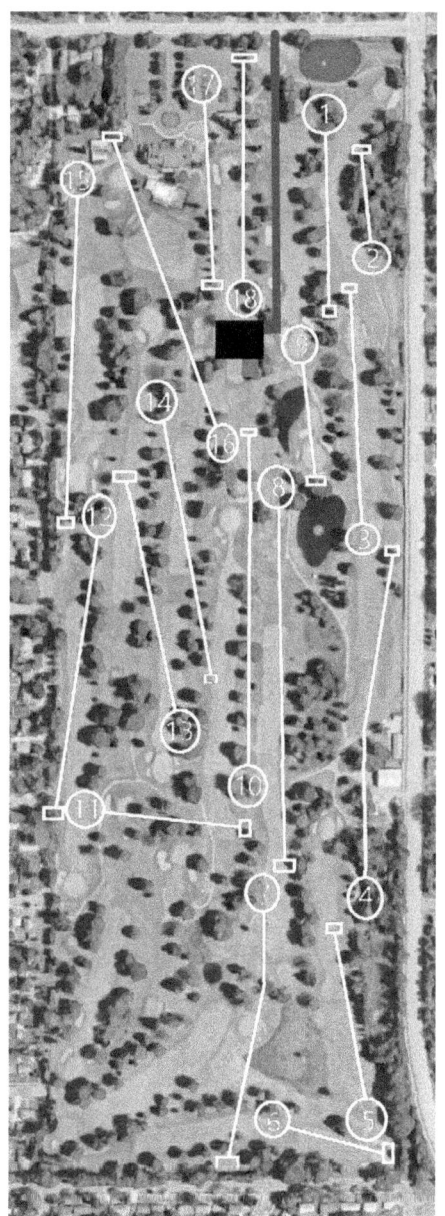

Hillcrest Golf Club's 2017 routing, superimposed with the routing of Lakeview/Hillcrest's original nine holes in 1921 plus the original proposed routing of a second nine. For reference, Larpenteur Avenue is the street at the top of the photo.

GRAPHIC COURTESY
OF ROSS WALKOWIAK.

"ST. PAUL - LAKE PARK GOLF CLUB, THE.

"Located on West Como and Snelling Avenue."

This is a much-traveled intersection, with daily north-south traffic heavy on Snelling Avenue and even heavier in late summer, and the Minnesota State Fairgrounds at the northwestern corner of the intersection. Yet I would doubt even 0.007 percent of the folks who roll past on two or four wheels have the foggiest idea there was a golf course nearby (or probably would care, but to each their own).

The Lake Park Golf Club, relatively small in stature and as far as I can tell unremarkable in every other way, long ago and for maybe as little as one golf season occupied a thin, rectangular plot of land not quite at Como and Snelling but within a solid midiron strike of it.

Information on The Lake Park Golf Club is sketchy, beyond the confirmation that it did in fact exist. That can be found in the April 2, 1922, edition of the *St. Paul Pioneer Press*, within a short story about local indoor golf clubs shutting down for the season in advance of the outdoor season. (Indoor golf clubs in downtown St. Paul and Minneapolis were common in the 1920s.) The story mentioned "Carl Lindgren, who again this season will be at the Lakeview Golf club and Sig Hanson who will teach the game at the newly organized Lake Park golf club."

Whether Lake Park survived into the 1923 season, I don't know. Sharon Shinomiya of *the Como Park Bugle* passed along this nugget, a passage from the *St. Paul Daily News* of April 1, 1923, in a story headlined "St. Paul Golf Clubs Prepare to Start Season Soon."

"Chelsea Heights is the only course that is in doubt about having an instructor, but as golf pros are not lacking, it is probable that Chelsea Heights will have one also. This is the new course that was opened last year at Como …"

The Chelsea Heights reference surely was to the Lake Park course, which was — depending on whose hairs you care to split regarding geographical designations — in the Chelsea Heights or Tilden area of St. Paul's Como neighborhood.

All indications are that The Lake Park Golf Club was an arm of something called the Lake Park Club, probably named for its proximity to Lake Como. A 1923 aerial photo of a plot just south of the southeast corner of Snelling and Como, just north of railroad tracks, shows what almost certainly was fairway routing and just enough room for a nine-hole golf course. The area now is occupied mostly by the Hmong College Prep Academy and Como Park Apartments.

CHAPTER 17

Rubik Was Here

More! Gone.

My head hurts.

Included on the facing page is a routing map for a Minnesota lost golf course, I won't say where or when. It has me more confused than the folks who used to start their round on Minneapolis Golf Club, got lost and wound up on the adjacent and now-abandoned Westwood Hills Golf Course in St. Louis Park, or vice versa (true story).

My thing is, if I'm looking at the routing map correctly, how was this course correctly navigated without the use of a hard hat or the threat of multiple personal injury lawsuits on any given day?

This was a nine-hole course that apparently could be played as an 18-holer. Along with the routing map came these notations:

"Here's an easy rule to remember where holes 10–18 are:

"For even numbered holes:
  Divide by 2

"So 10 is at 5

"12 is at 6

"18 is at 9 (which is at 4)

"For odd numbered holes:
  Subtract 10

"So 13 is at 3

"15 is at 5

"17 is at 7

"The only exception is: 11 is at 4

"P.S. Any questions, just ask
  (name redacted)."

I am not kidding about any of this.

I spent about 10 minutes looking at the map. Not going to spend any more time on it, not going to try to contact (redacted) for further explanation. I did figure out that some, maybe all, greens had to be used twice during an 18-hole round.

I have little doubt there's an explanation that even I could understand, but I don't see it. All I know is that the lines intersect 62 times, if my count is right ...

... and my head hurts.

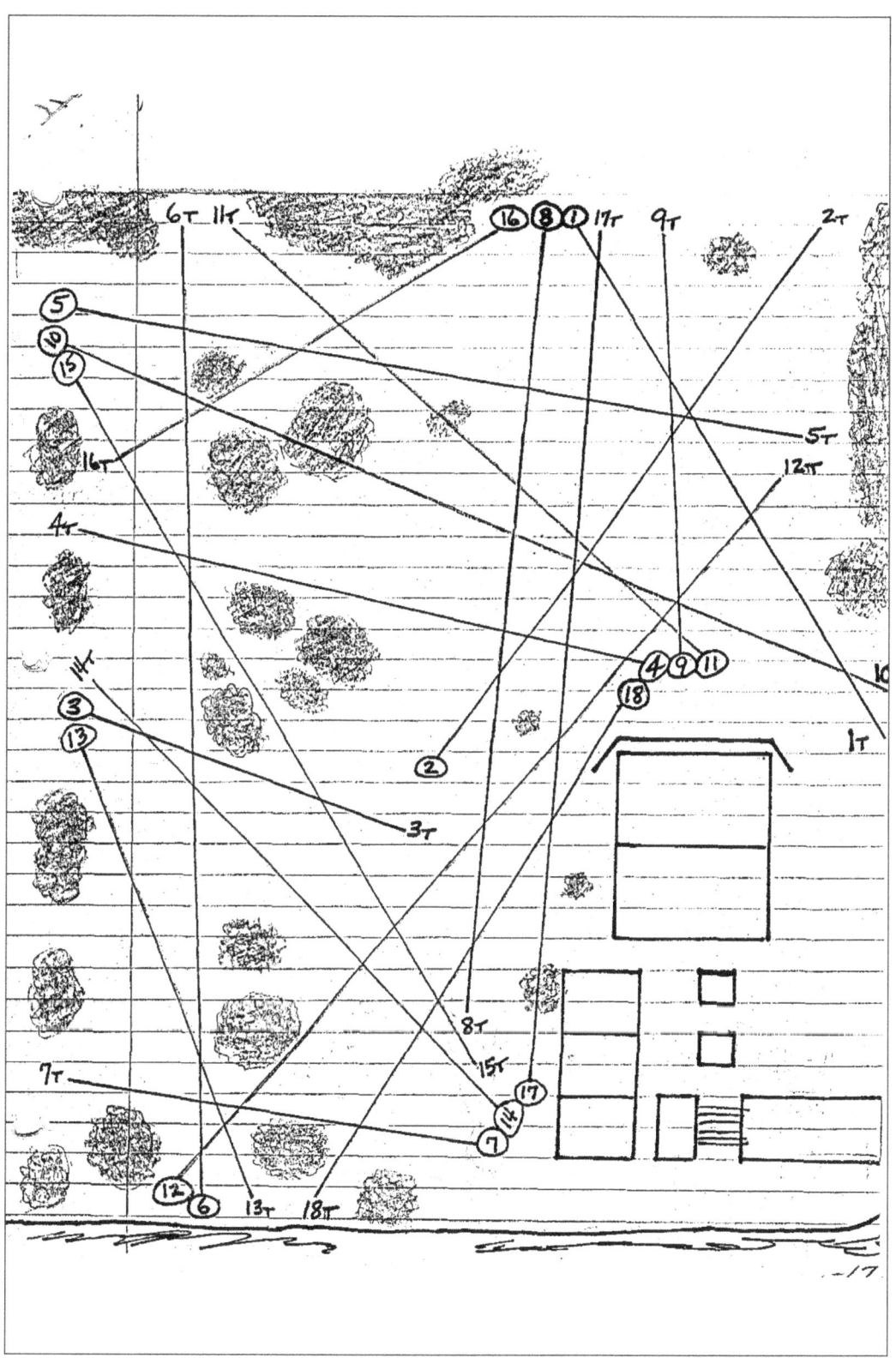

CHAPTER 18
The Hastings Bridge

*"I got a hole in one there.
Right there."*

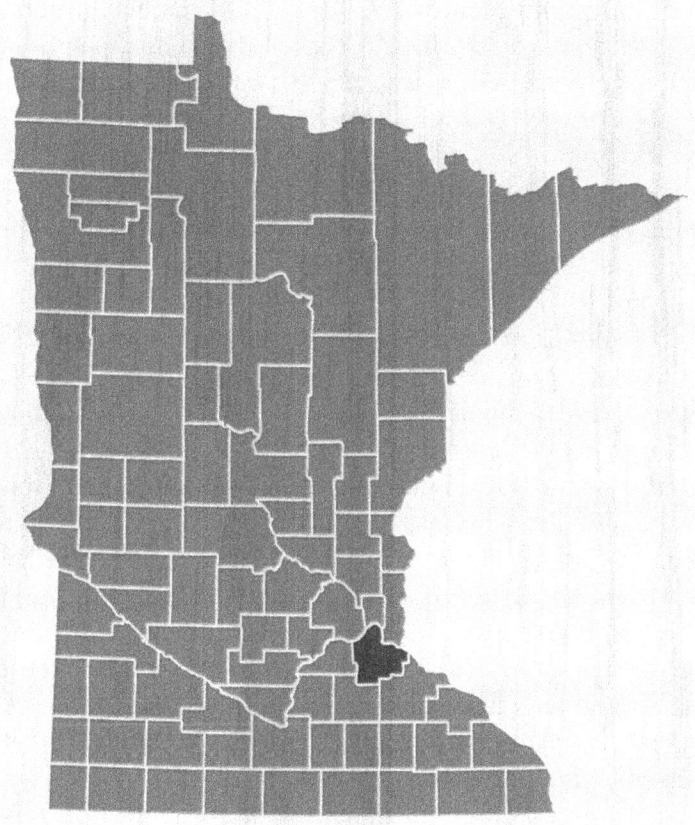

**COURSE: VALLEY VIEW GOLF COURSE
CITY: HASTINGS
COUNTY: DAKOTA
YEARS: 1929–60**

More! Gone.

AUG. 31, 2015

In eight days, school will be back in session at John F. Kennedy Elementary in Hastings, and the golf course will again be treated with reckless disregard and utter impunity.

First-graders will run screaming across the greens. Third-graders will jump and stomp and kick at the fairways as if they weren't even there. Recess monitors will look away, as if nothing untoward were happening. Custodians, in the ultimate show of indifference, will toss garbage all about the George Nelson Historical Monument.

If they only knew ...

... yeah, they would just keep doing it.

Understandable. Hey, all the kids see is a schoolyard. Play on.

A few others — very few anymore — also see an old golf course on the Kennedy grounds. Decades ago, a course known as Valley View, which went by other names later in life, occupied what is now the schoolyard, along with part of the current Smead Manufacturing site and undeveloped land to the south and east.

As a golf course site, this tract isn't particularly notable. There are few elevation changes, no water and no overly distinguishing features. As a bridge, however, the site carries significance.

And in Hastings, bridges (think Spiral Bridge, 1895–1951; "Big Blue" High Bridge, 1951–2013; and four-laner, 2013-present) are a big deal.

Valley View spanned all or parts of 31 golf seasons in Hastings and bridged a gap between a mostly unknown era of golf in the city, going all the way back to 1924, and the present day.

Oh, yeah. About that monument ...

George Nelson, 84, and his friend Bill McNamara, 81, both Hastings residents and former golfers at the Valley View site, rode along one warm August afternoon as I went to visit the place. I turned south from 10th Street East onto Tyler Street. We hung a quick left into the main Kennedy Elementary parking lot and proceeded directly and purposefully across ... um, the old first fairway.

We veered right, into the school's east parking lot, and Nelson spotted the monument.

"I got a hole in one there," he said. "Right there."

"Right there," meaning at a corner of the east parking lot and on the exact site of the old No. 2 green at Valley View (and I mean exact, going off old aerial photos). There lies a large steel marker, paying tribute to the ace Nelson recorded 66 years ago while representing Hastings in a high school golf match.

Well, maybe that's a stretch. The George Nelson Historic Monument ... is a Dumpster. It is the site of Nelson's 1949 hole in one at the Hastings course.

The Dumpster was, of course, not there in 1949 when Nelson pulled a 6-ion from his bag, teed off from a slight rise by where the Kennedy playground now stands, aimed north, landed the ball just short of the green because, he said,

The Hastings Bridge

George Nelson, left, and Bill McNamara in August 2015 stand near the site of the second tee at the former Valley View Golf Course site in Hastings, now home to the John F. Kennedy Elementary School grounds. Nelson aced this second hole in 1949, holing out his tee shot to the green, which lay near the Dumpster at the corner of the school building in the background.

JOE BISSEN PHOTO

that was the only way you could successfully play holes with sand greens, and watched it hop and roll into the hole.

"We had so much fun out here," Nelson said to McNamara, which was easy for him to say considering he once had the distinct pleasure of penciling in a "1" on his scorecard.

Nelson and McNamara spent the better part of an hour showing me around the grounds, pointing out where every hole was, 1 through 9, and reminiscing. They were preserving the bridge.

Hastings Gazette, July 25, 1924. Headline: Golf Course Assured For Fans Of City.

"Arrangements whereby the sporting element of Hastings will soon be able to gratify their desires for outdoor recreation, were revealed here this week in the announcement that the use of a natural golf course on the Nick Conzemius farm a mile west of the city has been secured by local enthusiasts of the sport.

"The proposed course, starting at the western boundary line of the city proper, extends for fully a mile in a westerly direction and abounds in hazards that should test the bility (sic) of golfers in this vicinity to their hearts' content it is stated by those who have examined the proffered grounds."

Well, that's a mouthful and then some.

This original Hastings golf club, which was given no formal name in the newspaper story, had an initial member-

More! Gone.

The Valley View Golf Course clubhouse, circa 1930.

ship of 25; membership fee was $1. The course consisted of nine holes. Best guess is that the course was near what is now Conzemius Park and Hastings Middle School.

Five years later, the club moved east, according to an entry in *The Hastings Archives*, by Richard B. Darsow. "1929: The Valley View Golf Course, formerly on the Nick Conzemius Farm, was moved and laid out on the Fred C. Gillitt farm, corner of Tenth and Tyler Streets."

Whomever first wrote about Valley View at the Gillitt site for the *Hastings Gazette* veritably swooned over the place, which wasn't unusual for community newspaper writers of the day. I don't know, maybe there was a set of shiny, new hickory-shafted MacGregors in it for the author.

"There are few golf courses in the country that excel the Valley View grounds in natural beauty or commanding location," the *Gazette* reported on July 26, 1929, a month before the course officially opened. From the first green, the newspaper continued, "the golfer commands a magnificent view of both the Mississippi and Vermillion valley and the distant hills of Wisconsin, some of which are perhaps 10 miles away." (The view is today obscured by building construction and tree canopies.)

Bluster aside, the Valley View site had staying power, even through tough times of the Great Depression and World War II. The golf course lasted through 1949, when club members voted 24–12 not to sell the land to an interested private party.

But in 1957, feeling squeezed by residential growth and looking for room to perhaps expand to 18 holes, members began exploring potential new sites. They found one just over a mile to the southwest. On Sept. 2, 1958, the club purchased the John P. Zweber farm, and on May 1, 1961, Hastings Country Club opened with nine holes off Westview Drive, just a few blocks south of the old Conzemius Farm site. A second nine opened in 1966. (Update, 2020: After a brief dormancy in 2015, the course reopened. It now operates as Hastings Golf Club & Events.)

Meanwhile, the Valley View site at the Gillitt farm is a lost course. Gone, but 55 years later, not entirely forgotten.

At the southeast corner of 10th and Tyler stands the Community Education building for Hastings Schools. This is the site of the former clubhouse for Valley View/ Hastings Golf Club/ Hastings Country Club. The clubhouse originally was a two-story home owned by Gillitt, judging by the 1929 Gazette story on Valley View.

Just to the east, near the corner of 10th and Bailey, was Valley View's first

The Hastings Bridge

Bill McNamara, left, and George Nelson stand on the railroad tracks that divided the five western opening holes at Valley View from its four eastern closing holes.

JOE BISSEN PHOTO

tee. The opening hole headed south, with the green near a corner of the Kennedy grounds, up a small hill and near the school's playground.

McNamara grew up across 10th Street from the first tee, having moved there as a 12-year-old in 1946. "My aunt Martha Yanz got me started playing with her, and so a life of frustration was born!" he wrote in an e-mail after our visit to the site.

Nelson, who played the course almost daily, he said, remained a Hastings Country Club member when the new course opened in 1961. He is no longer a member there. McNamara did not make the transition to the current Hastings CC site, though he still plays area courses with a group of retirees.

"Living so close," McNamara wrote in his e-mail, "we kids made the course our own. Golf and ballgames in the summer, skating and sliding on the hills in the winter. My dad cut grass and did maintenance in his spare time, and even did a little golfing."

Of the course, he wrote: "A short distance, by today's standards, nine holes, with SAND GREENS, small, hard, oiled sand, flat as a pancake. No water hazards or sand traps, unless you count the greens!

"... It was our course, and we loved it."
George Nelson died in 2019 at age 87.

CHAPTER 19

Antiques Quiz Show

*"... if the common rabble
will go out there some evening
now they will hear some expressions like
caddie, tee, hazards, bunkers, putter,
cleek, niblick etc."*

**COURSE: YOU'LL SEE
COUNTY: YOU'LL SEE
YEARS: I SAID YOU'LL SEE**

More! Gone.

Twenty questions about Minnesota golf history, minus 19:

Which city in western Minnesota was the first to have a golf course?

I'll give you 50 guesses, and I'll bet you a beat-up Dunlop you won't guess right.

OK, try this. I'll hand you a cheat sheet of all Minnesota cities (just imagine that I did), Ada to Zumbrota, and ask you to guess. Probably, you'll say, a fairly large city — Bemidji, maybe. Moorhead, Alexandria, Marshall ... you get the idea. Or maybe something medium-sized: Fairmont, Redwood Falls, Detroit Lakes, Worthington.

Wrong on all counts.

Ada to Zumbrota, remember? Except it can't be Zumbrota, because Z-ville isn't even in western Minnesota. ...

... which brings us to the starting point ...

... Ada.

Ada, as in bingo. The first Minnesota golf course west of St. Cloud, from everything I have gathered, belonged to Ada, a small Norman County city close to — well, not so much of anything except maybe the neighboring city of Borup, the North Dakota border and some rich wheat-producing soil.

Why Ada? Those might be six of the most puzzling letters in Minnesota golf history.

"And now Ada has a club devoting itself to the 'Royal and Ancient game called Goff,'" the *Norman County Herald* reported on July 31, 1900. "... The links are in Hampson's addition and if the common rabble will go out there some evening now they will hear some expressions like caddie, tee, hazards, bunkers, putter, cleek, niblick etc. But they say golf is a royal game for steady people."

Quite the backhanded compliment, if you ask me.

Anyway, the *Herald* story, plus a reprint in the Aug. 2, 1900, *Minneapolis Tribune* listed the club's members: Rev. Styles, Messrs. and Mesdames Walter Topp, C.C. Allen, George Hosmer, Theodore Tenny and C.R. Andrews. The Hampson's addition reference was to an area just east and northeast of downtown Ada that now includes East Side Park. I don't know whether the old golf course lay where the park does now.

Ada very possibly came by its status as a golf pioneer honestly. The city, local historian Solveig Kitchell explained in a phone conversation, was first settled by a Scotsman, and most of its early residents were of Scottish and Irish origins. And "the game called Goff," of course, had similar origins.

Also, Ada's population in 1900 was 1,253, substantial enough to have supported a golf club.

It appears, however, that Ada's first golf course was as long-lasting as a stick of Juicy Fruit. I found no other references to the golf club in subsequent 1900 issues of the *Norman County Herald*, nor in scrolling through many issues of the 1901 and 1902 *Herald* and *Norman County Index*.

Golf in Ada, then, perhaps lay fallow for nearly the next three decades. Then it sprang back to life.

"May Have Golf Course," read a Page 1 headline in the *Index* of April 17, 1930. The story described steps being taken by a group of Ada residents, chaired by Rev. L.C. Jacobson, to form a local golf club.

On May 1, 1930, the *Index* offered more details on the new Ada Golf Club. It reported that arrangements had been made to lease land for six holes on the Norman County Fairgrounds property, with the "other three by the southwest on the Thorpe land." An additional four to five acres adjoining on the west of the fairgrounds land were to be used for golf, except during county fair time, when it would serve as a parking lot.

A 1916 plat map of Ada shows the Norman County Fairgrounds on the southwestern corner of the city. The map also shows significant amount of land owned by Thorpes. Garrett L. Thorpe was a prominent citizen in early Ada; Google searches reveal he was manager of Thorpe Produce and Thorpe Elevator, that he owned 5,500 acres in Norman County in 1903, that he had been a Union soldier in the Civil War and Democratic Party figure and game and fish commissioner, and that he was a Hereford and racehorse breeder.

"A professional in laying out golf courses is expected to arrive next week," the *Index* reported. "... Local golfers of experience believe that the site selected is ideal for the purpose, being close to the city, and containing plenty of hazards." The club had nearly 40 members, the newspaper reported — a rather large contingent for small-town clubs of that era.

The professional did indeed arrive the next week. The *Index* reported that the course had been laid out by Fargo, N.D., professional Ralph Kingsrud, at the behest of club member S.J. Skaurud. Kingsrud was a prominent figure in North Dakota golf. He was the pro at Fargo Country Club, played in the 1928 U.S. Open and was inducted into the North Dakota Golf Hall of Fame in 1977.

Ada Golf Club had at least a few good years. The *Minneapolis Tribune* reported on April 17, 1932, that the club had 83 members, was expected to have 100 by the end of the year, and that an expansion to 18 holes was on the horizon. (I found no evidence that that ever happened.) The *Index* reported on April 14 that the club had in 1931 "enjoyed another successful year ... a cash flow of $71 on hand after purchasing considerable equipment in the past year." The highest fee for club membership was $10 a year, and green fees were 50 cents on weekdays and 50 cents for each nine played on Sundays and holidays.

In May 1932, the club staged an 18-hole, medal-play tournament. In cold and windy weather, Oscar Bang headed the field of 14 players with a 41–40—81. In September, the club planned a members-only tournament, but it was rained out and apparently never rescheduled.

Sometime after that, Ada Golf Club began losing its shine. In June 1937, the *Index* reported that "efforts will be made to re-organize (the club) for this year, if enough interest is shown in the project. ... The local course is in good shape and could be maintained but with little expense."

A week later, the *Index* reported that "the local course will be maintained again this season" and that membership would be $5. Presumably, the 50 percent price reduction from five years earlier can be attributed to the effects of the Great Depression.

But in searching through much of the *Norman County Herald* from 1938, I found no mention of the local club or course.

Whether 1937 was the end of Ada Golf Club, I don't know. But golf again returned to the city in 1960 with a third course, Heart of the Valley, on the southeastern edge of town and still in operation.

Late to the Party — Barely

Ada earned its historic western Minnesota status by only 10 months. In May 1901, short-lived golf clubs were established in Fergus Falls and Marshall. Like Ada, both cities would later have successive lost courses. There are deep dives on both cities' lost courses in ForeGoneGolf.com, but here are the highlights:

Marshall: On May 17, 1901, the *Marshall News Messenger* posted this: "The golf craze is about to hit Marshall, and will probably hit it hard. A number of would-be golfers who don't as yet know a golf stick from a hay rake have been talking golf the past week and are now preparing enthusiastically to order outfits and lay out a ground — or is it 'green' or 'links.' The ground now being considered is on the east side of the river, and nine links will be made to start with. ... Soon the members will be wrestling with the golfer's jargon, and the uninitiated will be wondering at foozles, bunkers, tees, drives, caddies, etc."

A *News Messenger* story from the next week placed the grounds as "the railroad land on each side of the Northwestern, beyond the Marshall Milling Company's plant." My interpretation is that this would be near where the Lyon County Sheriff's Office is now — which is west of the Redwood River, not east of it.

On Aug. 9, 1901, the newspaper reported this: "The golf links continue to attract a number of golfers every day and evening. Bert Welsford has lowered the score twice this week, putting the best score yet made on the course at 57, most of the golfers playing around 75."

I did not find any stories on the course at this site beyond 1901.

Golf reappeared in Marshall in 1924 on a site not far away. The course measured 2,792 yards. A new nine holes opened in 1941 on the southwest side of town, where the current 18-hole Marshall Golf Club lies.

Fergus Falls: The *Fergus Falls Daily Journal* announced the arrival of organized golf in town on May 2, 1901. "A number of golf players have been out nearly every evening, and the game promises to be a very popular one during the coming summer," the newspaper reported.

The course appears to have existed only for that season. The *Journal* placed the course as being in the northeastern part of the city, near "the Jefferson school building," though other reports placed it in the southwestern part of town.

Golf re-emerged in 1922 with a nine-hole course on a 65-acre site along the south bank of the Otter Tail River and just west of what is now Hillcrest Lutheran Academy. Robert Overgaard caddied there as a youth and recalled working for a fellow named Tomhave who was the club's best player despite using only irons.

"I caddied for Tomhave, and he used me as sort of a rabbit's foot," Overgaard said by phone from Fergus Falls. "I had a butch, and the first time I ever caddied for him he had a real good score, and so after that, he wanted me to caddie. He'd rub my head and say, 'Hey, come over here, I got a tough shot here' and he'd rub my butch haircut."

That site is presumed to have been abandoned around 1940, and in 1941, Pebble Lake Golf Course, designed by Paul Coates, opened along the southwestern shore of Pebble Lake. It remains in operation.

CHAPTER 20

Back to the '50s, and a Naked Truth

"One of the things about the 1950s is that you didn't need a whole lot of money to play golf. Guys were playing in Army fatigues and white T-shirts."

COURSE: ALBERT LEA COUNTRY CLUB
CITY: ALBERT LEA
COUNTY: FREEBORN
YEARS: 1912–2006

More! Gone.

Albert Lea Country Club, born 1912 passed away 2006, holds a position of prominence as a pioneering Minnesota golf course. It ranks roughly among the first 20 to 25 organized sites in the state upon which were struck smother-hooked drives and fat approach shots. In southeastern Minnesota, only Winona, Rochester and Faribault had golf courses before Albert Lea Country Club opened for business, pre-World War I, in a clubhouse that was a converted horse barn.

Albert Lea Country Club survived — nay (or neigh, to lamely pursue horse barn references), thrived — through 95 years. Its shortstop was long one of southern Minnesota's prime tournaments, at one time attracting fields approaching 200 players. One notable winner was 1957 champion John Eymann of Forest City, Iowa, who played golf cross-handed.

Albert Lea Country Club grounds and clubhouse.
L.L. COOK CO. POSTCARD

And like any golf course worth its weight in either gold or just plain auld sod, Albert Lea Country Club created memories.

Dex Westrum spent much of his youth at Albert Lea Country Club in the 1950s.

"One of the things about the 1950s is that you didn't need a whole lot of money to play golf," Westrum said in a 2017 phone interview. "Guys were playing in Army fatigues and white T-shirts. For people that were just hackers, they could buy five irons, two woods, a putter and a cheap 50 cent golf ball and have a wonderful time. Now they've got to spend thousands of dollars."

Westrum is a retired college professor who lives in South Milwaukee, Wis., and is the son of the late Lyle Westrum. The latter was the professional at Albert Lea Country Club for a short time in the 1950s after having caddied there in the 1930s, going off to World War II, then returning after the war and turning professional upon finishing second in the Albert Lea shortstop. Lyle Westrum, his son noted, also had been a prominent Albert Lea hockey player and all-conference fullback in football.

Young Dexter Westrum followed his father onto the golf course in the 1950s. Among his memories of life at Albert Lea Country Club:

"After the war, there was a great interest in golf," Dex Westrum said, "and a lot of women, if they wanted to spend time with their husbands, they took lessons. He (Lyle Westrum) had 12 to 15 lessons a day, and most if not all of them were to women. Men would prefer to do it their way."

Albert Lea CC's many sand bunkers presented hazards for its golfers. The driving range presented a hazard for young Dex.

"Lesson balls had to be shagged, and I was elected to stand in the practice fairway collecting balls in a shag bag while the people took aim at me," Westrum says in reading from a passage he penned for *Minnesota Memories 2*, written and compiled by Joan Claire Graham. "Once in a while I would lose sight of a ball in the sun and get hit. But fortunately, most people couldn't hit the ball straight until the lesson was over.

"I received 40 cents for a half-hour lesson, which resulted in quite a sum by the end of the day. I immediately spent half of my earnings at the Ben Franklin store on new comic books. I eventually had more than 300 comics, which my mother threw away shortly after I left (Albert Lea)...."

Westrum recalled a relaxed atmosphere surrounding golf in the 1950s, with ladies days on Tuesdays and Wednesday men's days including steak dinners after a round of golf.

Another notable experience took place every year on the Albert Lea CC grounds.

"The highlight every summer was the Fourth of July, because the country club was where the fireworks were shot off," Westrum said in reading from *Minnesota Memories 2*. "The whole town turned out, cars lining up on old Highway 13 along No. 3 and the driveway along No. 4. People sat elbow to elbow along No. 7 hill. ...

"Best of all, there was free ice cream for all the kids. ... It was rich and it was cold, and one dip was plenty. In the morning, caddies would find cardboard remnants of the fireworks. Sometimes they found them in the bushes by the clubhouse. One year, there was a bunch of stuff on the clubhouse roof."

Dare it be said that one of Westrum's ALCC memories tops all others.

"The Edgewater (Cottage) was so close to No. 7, it provided my father with a challenge on the morning after the high school prom in 1961," Westrum wrote for the memories book. "He went to take the dew off the greens so they could be mowed when he discovered two naked teenage lovers on the green. Fortunately, he was more than a hundred yards away when he saw them. He didn't want to embarrass them or himself, so he went back to the pro shop, picked up his wedge and practice ball bag and returned to hit balls at them from a safe distance until they woke up and ran on."

Albert Lea Country Club fostered some excellent players in those days. The 1952 high school team won the state championship (as did the 1982 team). Individual state champions from Albert Lea included Clayton "Bumper" Westrum (Dex's uncle, 1950 and '52, and later the designer of the Northern Hills course in Rochester), Craig Clauson (1954), Dex's teammate Dick Jones (1962), Mark Knutson (1973) and Chad Adams (1989). On the girls side, Donna Boom won a state title in 1994.

The old Albert Lea Country Club course required shotmaking. Dex Westrum relates a memory from the shortstop:

"Neil Croonquist (two-time State Amateur champion) and some of the other guys who were playing decent amateur golf in the Twin Cities, they came down and they did not tear that Country Club course apart," Westrum said in the phone interview. "It wasn't long, but it was really hilly and had very

More! Gone.

Dex Westrum shows fine form in playing a shot from one of the "yawning traps," as he referred to them, as a youth at Albert Lea Country Club. The bunker was on No. 6; the shot was observed by Dick Davies Jr., and Westrum says the ball finished within a foot of the hole.

PHOTO COURTESY DEX WESTRUM

small greens. You miss the hole by 30 feet in Minneapolis, you got a 30-foot putt. You miss the hole by 30 feet in Albert Lea and you're in the trap."

One year, Westrum said, "Neil Croonquist was medalist with 69; nobody else broke par. ... Bud Chapman ... a hell of a good player. He came down to the Albert Lea shortstop, and he qualified for the fifth flight. That was the year the wind blew and it took something like 83 or 82 to make the championship flight. He came back the next year and won the tournament to distinguish himself, and he never came back."

The Albert Lea HS team that Westrum played on as a junior and senior featured Jones and four others who could break 40 for nine holes, he said. "So we were a formidable lot. In fact, I don't think we ever lost a home match. ... Teams would come and play us, and they just couldn't handle the uneven lies. There were hardly any holes where you were going to hit off a flat surface."

Westrum went off to college, then to a teaching career that covered 50 years, 10 schools and five states. His final memory of Albert Lea Country Club comes from the pages of *Minnesota Memories 2*:

"On my first visit back to Albert Lea Country Club after I heard the course was going to be destroyed, I took my 7-year-old son ... for a walk on the old holes 7, 8 and 9. Stakes all over the landscape marked what I assumed were planned housing sites. This is where I was a little boy and where I was a high school kid.

"I tried to explain what the holes looked like in the 1950s and 1960s and that the course had been one of the most distinctive nine-hole layouts in Minnesota. It had small greens, narrow fairways and sand traps you could get lost in.

"I never saw the additional nine or played another version of the course after the final high school meet of the 1963 season against Red Wing."

CHAPTER 21
Unheard of

"The Most FASCINATING and SCENIC PLAYGROUND That Has Ever Been Opened to the Public."

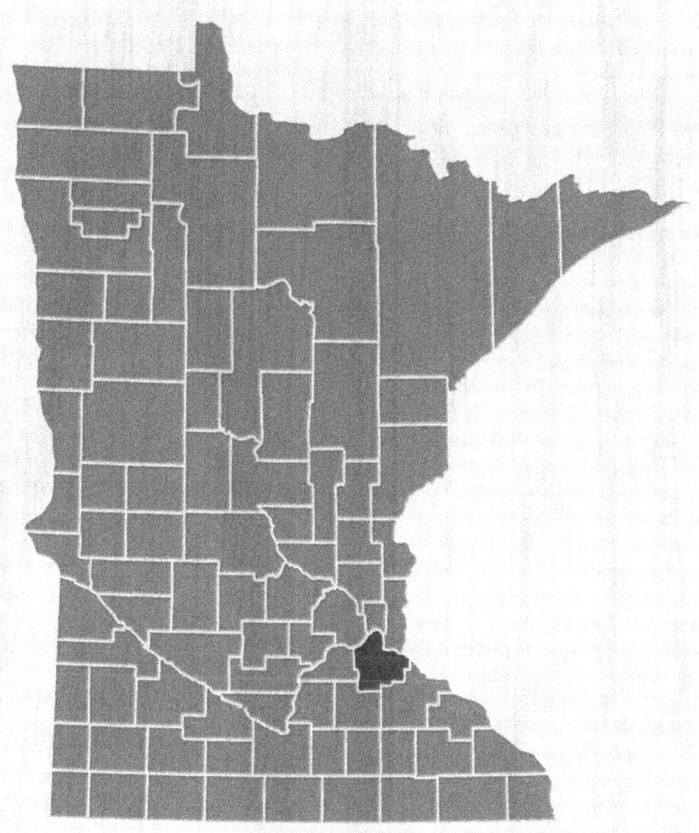

COURSE: ORCHARD BEACH AND GOLF CLUB
CITY: LAKEVILLE
COUNTY: DAKOTA

More! Gone.

SEPTEMBER 2018

On a warm September afternoon, sunny and calm and a blue-ribbon day for golf, I drive south on I-35E, through Burnsville, past the freeway's east-west merger onto I-35, past Buck Hill Ski Area, take the next exit and find myself in Lakeville.

I hop off the freeway, head south a half-mile, and pull into the spot where the clubhouse is.

Or was, I guess.

I know it should be here, on this very spot, because I have studied this area closely online for more than a year.

Only … no clubhouse. Instead, the sign on the door reads:

"Chipotle."

Thrown off, I stop to regroup. I walk in the door and stride up to the counter.

Me: "Can I just have a small soda?"
Worker: "Two dollars and four cents."
Me: "And the 2:44 tee time."
Pause.
Worker: "Sorry?"
Me: "Never mind."

I got the soda. Not the tee time.

Then again, no one ever did.

Burrito bowls and carnitas were not what Leo Harmon had in mind for this portion of northwestern Lakeville when, more than 90 years ago, he and/or his business partners took out a series of ads in the *Minneapolis Tribune*.

"Orchard Beach and Golf Club," read the large type in an October 1926 ad. In smaller type, the ad crowed: "The Most FASCINATING and SCENIC PLAYGROUND That Has Ever Been Opened to the Public."

Well, then.

Hyperbole has always been a staple in golf-course promotion. This was hyperbole, Roaring Twenties style, on performance-enhancing substances.

Harmon, a Michigan logging entrepreneur and banker, took out another ad that ran in the June 11, 1927, issue of the *Tribune*, occupying two-thirds of a page. "ANNOUNCING," it read, "The Most Unique Club in the Northwest …"

The ad featured a map of the southeastern corner of Orchard Lake and the surrounding area. Routing for an 18-hole golf course is shown, each hole plain as day. The first, 18th and half of the 17th holes were to be on the eastern side of railroad tracks that coincidentally led three miles southeast to Antlers Park, where in the 1920s and '30s George O'Rourke operated a well-known amusement park and golf course (both long since abandoned).

On the far right side of the map, a flagpole is depicted, with a building nearby and the designation "Golf Club House." Those three words are printed right about where today you can order extra sour cream or guacamole for your Chipotle taco.

But the flagpole, it is presumed, was never erected, the flag was never raised, and Orchard Beach and Golf Club instead ranks as the most unheard-of and mysterious lost-golf course site (almost-lost, to be perfectly accurate) I have come across.

The June 1927 ad was one of at least a dozen for Orchard Beach that ran in the *Tribune* that year. Some advertised the magnificent spectacle that would be Orchard Beach and Golf Club; others were aimed at recruiting a sales force. Orchard Beach would be unlike anything Twin Citians had ever seen. And it wasn't just golf and a lake that were proffered. Other ads and newspaper stories promised tennis, playgrounds, an athletic field, parks, an aviation field and a large residential development — all situated, according to an October 1926 ad, "amid rolling hills generously wooded with the virgin growth of beautiful hardwood trees and a myriad of the various wild flowers painted by Dame Nature."

Orchard Beach — the club, golf course and housing development — was to have encompassed an area that is loosely bordered, in 2020 terms, by Kenwood Trail on the east, 172nd Street West on the north, the southeast corner of Orchard Lake on the northwest and 185th Street West on the south. The western border likely includes parts of at least three holes on what is now Brackett's Crossing Country Club (established 1961).

The surf 'n' turf that was to be Orchard Beach and Golf Club never worked out. No tee time was ever reserved, no ace served, no seesaw seen, no aerial landing landed. I can find no documentation of the project dating to 1928 or later, and the project is so unknown that one might as well suggest the Loch Ness monster once inhabited Orchard Lake as to suggest there ever were big plans for the neighborhood. I contacted or tried to contact three historical societies, one courthouse and at least a dozen residents or former residents of the area, including at least three parties who live smack-dab on top of what was to be the golf course, and never heard so much as a whisper of knowledge of the Orchard Beach project.

Yet the current lie of the land indicates site work was started, and documents confirm it.

"A sporty 18 hole golf course is under construction," read part of a June 1927 ad in the *Minneapolis Tribune*. That same month, the *Tribune* ran a story headlined "Orchard Club Will Feature Recreation."

"Approximately 1,000 acres of land are being developed for the Orchard Beach and Golf Club, on Lyndale avenue south, 17 miles from Minneapolis," the story read. "The project is planned as one of the most completely equipped private recreational grounds in the northwest. The work has been under way since last fall."

Historic aerial photos support the notion that work was started and land cleared on the immense development but never finished. A closer look is available by visiting ForeGoneGolf.com.

Why couldn't Orchard Beach and Golf Club make a go? Opportunity seemed ripe, considering the strong U.S. economy of the mid-1920s, and the project was ambitious but the goal sensible: to build a golf-and-housing development less than 20 miles from downtown Minneapolis.

Yet Orchard Beach lasted less than two years and carved onto the Lakeville landscape little more than one small building, a couple of roads and a few strips of cleared land.

It's a mystery to me.

Orchard Beach and GC presumably was the brainchild of Leo Clinton Harmon, who left his positions of stature in Michigan's Upper Peninsula to move to Minnesota in 1926. A former bank president, lumber magnate and entrepreneur (shoes, leather, electricity and baby carriages, among other ventures), Harmon left the small city of manistique in '26 and, according to a resume' held by the Gulliver (Mich.) Historical Society, "moved to Minneapolis to engage in some special reorganization work for the Backus-Brooks Co., and the International Paper Company."

Marilyn Fischer, president of the Gulliver HS, wrote in correspondence that Harmon is considered one of the "Great Men in Manistique's History," purportedly even having first devised the use of white safety stripes on highways.

If there were motives for Harmon, at age 54, to emerge from the northern Michigan forest, where he presumably was wealthy and at least regionally renowned, and move to Minnesota, they are unclear. There is record of him having visited St. Paul on a business trip in 1924; its exact aims are unknown. But at some point, he turned his eyes toward a wooded, lakeside plot in Lakeville, at the time a small town of only about 500.

In October 1926, Harmon, along with Charles R. Hutchenson and M.P. LaFleur of Minneapolis, established Minnesota Lakes Inc. Real Estate, with a charter in Delaware. Hutcheson's background is unknown, but M.P. LaFleur presumably was Maynard Potter LaFleur, a World War I aviator and former professional hockey player from Eveleth, Minn., who was described in a 1982 *Minneapolis Tribune* story as a "real estate wheeler-dealer." He also was dubbed "the Duke of Marquette" because he owned so much land on Marquette Avenue in Minneapolis.

On March 7, 1927, a plat map covering part of the area near Orchard Lake in Lakeville was filed with Dakota County. The area was called Club Park Addition No. 1 of Orchard Beach and Golf Club and included features hearkening back to British literature: Tennyson Court, Burns Plaza, and streets named Longfellow, Byron, Emerson and Milton, among others. (Irony: Wasn't it Milton who wrote *Paradise Lost*?)

The first newspaper mention of Orchard Beach and Golf Club that I could find came in the June 11, 1927, edition of the *Minneapolis Tribune*, with a large advertisement detailing a proposed development with golfing, fishing, tennis, playgrounds and more — "An Ideal Family Private Playground. ... Now Being Organized." The ad featured a listing of advisory board members, with Harmon at the top:

"Mr. Leo C. Harmon, 185 Oak Grove St., Minneapolis, chairman, Inland Water Ways Commission; president of Tri-State Tractor Company; president of Minnesota Lakes, Inc. as sponsors of Orchard Beach and golf club; also president until recently of the First State Bank, Manistique, Michigan."

Among the nine other advisory board members were D.C. Bennett, Minneapo-

Two anglers cast for lunkers — or maybe just their next pan-fried lunch — on a late afternoon at the southeast corner of Orchard Lake Park in Lakeville. The spot coincides with access to Orchard Lake shown in a 1927 Minneapolis Tribune ad for the planned, but never completed, Orchard Beach Golf Club.

PETER WONG PHOTO

lis architect; Chris Whitman, manager of The Minikahda Club in Minneapolis (Minikahda Club records list Whitman as its manager from 1916–28); and James Corr of Minneapolis, an architect and civil engineer who was listed as surveyor of the Orchard Beach property in the aforementioned plat map.

The day after the ad appeared, the *Minneapolis Tribune* of June 12, 1927, published a short story headlined "Orchard Club Will Feature Recreation." "Approximately 1,000 acres of land are being developed for the Orchard Beach and Golf Club, 17 miles from Minneapolis," the story began. "A feature of the project will be an 18-hole golf course. Charles Harney of Chicago, amateur champion of upper Michigan, is here to lay out the course."

There is a possible Harney-Harmon connection here. Harney lived in Escanaba, Mich., an hour's drive from Harmon in Manistique, and won the 1921 Upper Peninsula Golf Association championship. The proposed routing of the Orchard Beach golf course, presumably executed by Harney, appears solid from a golf standpoint, and the prospects were promising, given the varied terrain.

I was unable, however, to find any evidence that Harmon ever did any other golf-course design work.

It appears likely that after Orchard Beach development started in 1926 or 1927, it stopped abruptly, maybe not even 10 percent in. The most plausible explanation is money, that Harmon and/or his investors ran into issues that killed the development. Yet I did find no verifiable indication of that.

Leo Harmon moved on from Minnesota. Quickly, it seems. The aforementioned resume' lists him as president of the Mid-West Tractor Company of Chicago from 1927–29. He moved to the Hearst Corporation, becoming assistant business manager of the *New York Evening Journal*, then moved to California sometime in the 1930s and died at age 80 on May 25, 1952, in Beverly Hills.

The mystery of Orchard Beach and Golf Club appears to have passed on as well.

CHAPTER 22

Central Hub

*"... the mecca of all
who have
the time to play."*

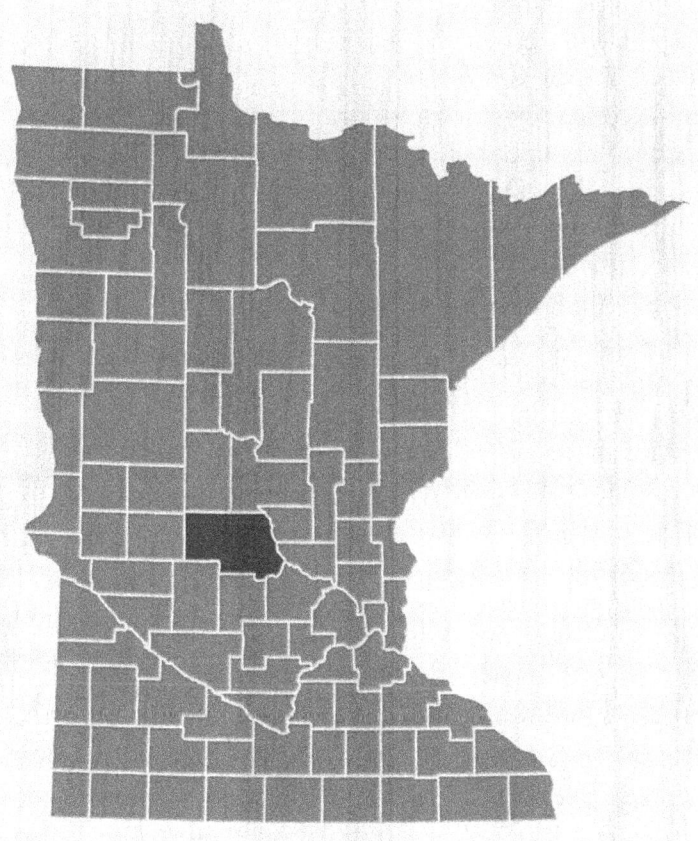

**COURSES: ST. CLOUD GOLF CLUB
AND OTHERS
COUNTY: STEARNS**

More! Gone.

St. Cloud, Minnesota, can accurately be described by either of two monikers. Choose your favorite:

"Granite City"

or

"Central Minnesota's Geographical Midpoint of Holy Cow That's a Ton of Lost Golf Courses"

Picked the first one, didn't you? Hard to argue. For one thing, "Granite City" does roll off the tongue easier than moniker No. 2. For another, the hard-and-durable construction rock — granite — has been harvested in and around St. Cloud since the 1880s, and, after all, golf in St. Cloud has been around "only" since 1899.

Yes, 1899. I'll get to it.

In 1928, as far as I can tell, there were only four golf courses within 30 miles of the Granite City: St. Cloud Country Club, established 1919; Little Falls Country Club, 1921; Clearwater CC at Annandale, 1925; and Princeton Golf Club at its fairgrounds site, 1928. I'm not including the short-lived campus course at St. John's in Collegeville (1925–33) or the apparently shorter-lived three- or six-hole concoction at Rockville (1926).

Then the floodgates opened. In the years 1929–32, a dozen more courses opened within that 30-mile radius. And then, quickly, the floodgates slammed shut. Eleven of the 12 were gone by 1945.

Here's a look, starting with a pre-1920 course that might come as a surprise to Granite Citians.

Not one and the same

St. Cloud Country Club, which nestles up against the Mississippi River on the south side of the Granite City, is one of Minnesota's classic old golf clubs. Established in 1919, it ranks among the first 35 or 40 clubs in state history. St. Cloud CC has hosted one men's State Amateur championship and two women's State Ams. The course was, by all accounts that I know of, designed by the redoubtable Tom Vardon.

But it was not St. Cloud's first golf course.

Take it from the May 10, 1899, edition of the *St. Cloud Daily Times*.

"NEW GOLF CLUB." read the headline, with the story following.

"A meeting of those interested in the game of golf was held last evening in the council chambers and the St. Cloud Golf Club was duly organized with 27 charter members," the newspaper reported. "... The membership fee was placed at $5. It is believed that a large number will become members of the new club as soon as the game is more thoroughly understood."

To be clear: St. Cloud Golf Club, established 1899, and St. Cloud Country Club, established 1919, were, judging by every piece of information I have come across, separate organizations in separate places. There might have been coincidental carryover from GC to CC in the form of members or maybe bylaws, but they were not the same golf club.

Two weeks before the formal inception of St. Cloud GC, the *Daily Times* had offered other details.

Headline, April 24: "GOLF LINKS LAID."

Story: "For some time the admirers of golf have been aggitating (sic) the formation of a club in this city and it is expected that such an organization will be formed this week.

"The links have been laid by Robert Foulis, of St. Paul, and he pronounces them as the equal of any in the cities, barring the fact that two railroad tracks are crossed here.

"The tee is located at the ball park, and the total length of the links are two and a fifth miles. From the tee to the first hole is 552 yards; to the second from this, 468; to the third, 250; fourth, 480; fifth, 512; sixth, 460; seventh, 296; eighth, 616; ninth, 360, making a total of 3,984 yards.

"The St. Cloud Golf club should start out with a large membership, and it undoubtedly will. O.H. Havill, Warren Freeman and H.R. Welsh are the promoters of the new club."

Digging into the details:

- The 1899 start date makes St. Cloud Golf Club one of Minnesota's first nine golf courses to have opened for play, matched or preceded, by my count, only by Town & Country Club and Roadside of St. Paul; Winona Golf Club and Meadow-Brook of Winona; Bryn Mawr, Minikahda and Camden Park of Minneapolis; and Northland of Duluth.

- The mention of Robert Foulis is significant. Foulis is a prominent figure from the first decade of Minnesota golf. A native Scotsman, he worked for the legendary Old Tom Morris at his shop in St. Andrews, then moved to the Chicago area in 1895 and to St. Paul in 1896 as the first professional at Minnesota's first golf course, Town & Country Club. Foulis' talents included swing instruction, clubmaking and course architecture. His design and redesign credits (some contributions are disputed) include Town & CC, Minikahda and the lost Bryn Mawr course in Minneapolis, Lake Forest (now Onwentsia) in the Chicago area and Bellerive in suburban St. Louis.

- The length of the St. Cloud Golf Club course is stunning. A nine-holer covering 3,984 yards, especially before the turn of the 20th century, would have been remarkably long, and a course with a longest hole of 616 yards and nothing shorter than 250 would be daunting even by today's standards.

As with so many lost courses, determining the course's location can be confusing, confounding and ultimately not 100 percent confirmable. Such is the case with St. Cloud GC, though with the help of three researchers at the Stearns County Museum and a few hours of sleuthing on the side, I am more than 95 percent certain of this:

St. Cloud Golf Club was situated near the western edge of the city, near its border with Waite Park and not far north of Division Street. Best guess is that the course opened near the intersection of what is now 3rd Street North and 37th Avenue, not far from BBC Park, and worked northward, eventually

BBC Park in northwest St. Cloud, near the presumed starting point of St. Cloud Golf Club.
JOE BISSEN PHOTO

crossing the railroad tracks and probably onto land that is now part of the former Electrolux plant.

I don't know how long St. Cloud Golf Club operated, though I'm thinking the year 1905 sounds about right. A 1901 *Minneapolis Journal* story notes that St. Cloud golfers would meet with those of Grand Forks, Fargo, Jamestown, Winnipeg and Duluth to organize the Northwestern Golf Association. Newspaper reports show that St. Cloud competed against Bryn Mawr in inter-club competitions in 1902. In July 1903, a *Minneapolis Journal* story reported that St. Cloud would be among the new clubs with competitors in the state tournament — but a story in August 1903 from the same newspaper said that St. Cloud was not a Minnesota Golf Association member. An MGA all-time membership roll from 1920 does not list St. Cloud Golf Club as ever holding membership.

A 1904-05 St. Cloud city directory lists St. Cloud Golf Club, with E.H. Hill as president and H.C. Ervin as secretary-treasurer. (Harry Ervin also was secretary-treasurer of the Tileston Milling Company.) But I could not find St. Cloud Golf Club in any newspaper mentions after 1903, and it was not mentioned in a 1910 city directory. The presumption is that the Country Club took up the torch for St. Cloud golf nine years later.

Outward

Using St. Cloud Golf Club as an unofficial hub of lost courses in the area, here are quick visits to others. More information on all of the St. Cloud-area lost courses can be found at ForeGoneGolf.com.

Wildwood Golf Course, 1929–circa 1931: Eight miles west of downtown St. Cloud lies the city of St. Joseph, prominently known as the home of the College of St. Benedict. (Yes, there are more Saints in Stearns County than on the favored side of the pearly gates.) And somewhere near St. Joseph, there once was a golf course.

"A lot of interest is being shown in the St. Joseph golf course," the *St. Cloud Times* reported on Aug. 2, 1929. "The nine hole course will be known as the Wildwood golf course. There are nine sporty holes with sand, green and fairways. This is something new for St. Joe and the outlook for a large membership is good."

Membership fee was $5, and a nine-hole greens fee cost 50 cents. "It looks good to go past the course which is located on the very edge of the village and see it dotted with enthusiasts," the *Times* article concluded.

The course appears to have not lasted past the 1931 season, and I failed to determine its exact location. Best guess: Judging by a 1938 aerial photo that may or may not show old golf course features, Wildwood could have been on a triangular plot just south of Millstream Park, on the western edge of St. Joseph.

Chain O' Lakes, Richmond, 1931–early 1940s: The 1929–31 Stearns County golf boom continued farther west with the establishment of a course in Richmond. The course was immediately to the southeast of the intersection of Highways 23 and 22.

The course was described as par–32, with a length of 3,205 yards (that's a long course for par 32).

Princeton Golf Club, 1928–29 and 1930–circa 1937: Golf in Princeton began with a six-hole course that lasted two seasons at the Mille Lacs County Fairgrounds. The next year, it moved to

A bend in the east branch of the Rum River in Princeton, near the southern edge of the Princeton Middle School grounds. The old Princeton Golf Club grounds likely lay near here and to the south, near Pioneer Park.

JOE BISSEN PHOTO

a tract on the north side of Princeton, near what is now Pioneer Park, with five holes on the west side of the Rum River (east branch) and four on the east. There is a very deep dive — brace yourself if you go there — at ForeGoneGolf.com into the mystery of trying to find the course's exact site. In the end, and with a couple of years' worth of hindsight, I have to wonder why organizers built a golf course on land that had to be prone to nasty flooding. The river's course has changed appreciably over the years, and much of the presumed golf course site now consists of back channels and swamp.

Mille Lacs County Golf Club, Foreston, 1929–31: This was something of a regional golf hub when it opened in 1929. The course consisted of nine holes on the riverbank, the *Mille Lacs County Times* reported, "a beautiful stretch of 52 acres, with sand greens, sand boxes, and benches at each tee." About 25 people played the course on

Opening Day, and the club had 25 members, with inaugural officers from the cities of Milaca, Princeton, Foley and Foreston.

"The riverbank" referred to the west branch of the Rum River, just south of where it passed under Minnesota Highway 23 — probably Old 23, not the current highway. The site was about a mile east of downtown Foreston.

In April 1931, the *St. Cloud Times* referred to the club as "the mecca of all who have the time to play."

In September 1931, the club hosted a five-county tournament, featuring players from Mille Lacs, Benton, Kanabec, Sherburne and Pine counties. I could find no record of the course being used in 1932 or later.

Milaca Golf Club, 1932–circa 1943: After the Foreston course was abandoned, it took mere months for a replacement to emerge.

Milaca Golf Club's course, 2.6 miles north of downtown Milaca, occupied land between the Rum River's east branch and what is now U.S. 169. Weekday greens fees were 25 cents. A 1932 *Mille Lacs County Times* story noted that the new course would have sand greens — one square, one octagonal and seven round. The layout was designed by a prominent figure in St. Cloud-area golf. Larry Rieder was a golf and football standout at St. Cloud Teachers College before becoming golf coach at the college and professional (and trick-shot artist) at St. Cloud Country Club.

Foley Golf Club, 1930–1936: The course was plotted on the Prudent Brunn farm, a half-mile south of downtown and close to the city's current course, Stone Creek. "Some of the fairways will be over sloping hills and among fine shade trees, and a small pond will provide a splendid water hazard," the *Foley Independent* reported in April 1930.

A playing lowlight, we must confess, was registered by Father Frank, then of St. Lawrence Catholic Church in nearby Duelm. The *Independent* of Sept. 24, 1930, reported on a tournament during the course's second month. Ernest Boberg had low score of the day, posting an even 100, "while Father First of Duelm developed bad eyes and had high score, it being 120."

The course likely was abandoned after the 1936 season.

St. Cloud Teachers College Course, 1931–1937: This six-hole course, across the Mississippi River to the east of the main campus of what is now St. Cloud State University, maintained a low-key existence for a half-dozen years in the 1930s. The *St. Cloud Times* of May 2, 1931, noted the university's acquisition of a six-block tract that came to be known as College Recreation Field, and the golf course likely was there, just north of where Selke Field is today.

"The plot just acquired will require but little in the way of improvements before ready for use," the Times noted. "The land is literally 'as flat as a table.'"

Benton County Golf Course, 1930–31: Another six-holer, this one occupied land on the county fairgrounds site in Sauk Rapids. It covered 1,800 yards, "is clean and sporty and with well-constructed greens and tee-offs," the *Times* reported in 1931. "The short holes are so situated as to allow interesting hazards and, in several instances, are more difficult than the longer ones."

Greens fees ranged from 25 cents per round on weekdays to 50 cents per day on Saturdays, Sundays and holidays.

Springbrook, St. Augusta, 1930s: Five miles south of downtown St. Cloud lies the city of St. Augusta, which sprawls across 30 square miles. In the north-central part of the city, not quite a mile north of the St. Augusta Fire Department headquarters and coincidentally the Hidden Lake Disc Golf Course, is a site upon which the targets were not steel baskets but 4 1/4-inch holes in the ground.

"St. Cloud's first public golf course, Springbrook, will be formally opened next Saturday and Sunday," the *St. Cloud Times* reported on April 30, 1930. "The name of the new course implies it's (sic) natural beauties. A little trout brook meanders through the entire property, necessitating two crossings during the course of a single round. Five pure water springs, giving up nearly ice cold water, are situated so that they are but a short distance from each of the nine holes."

The course was built on land owned by Charles H. Tanner, vice president of Northwestern Oil Company and a St. Cloud Country Club member. It opened with sand greens and in 1932 converted to grass but likely did not last long after that.

Scenic, Cold Spring, 1930–circa 1936: Cold Spring Golf Club was organized in 1930, and a seven-hole course was organized in Wakefield Township, 1.3 miles northwest of downtown and seven-tenths of a mile northwest of where Rocori High School is today. In 1931, the club leased 19 additional acres that was used to build two more holes and changed its name to "Scenic Golf Course."

A playing highlight of dubious sorts occurred on May 3, 1936. The *Times* reported on it the next day. "Ferdinand Peters, president of the Cold Spring Golf club, 'showed the boys how it was done' Sunday afternoon when he teed off and his ball struck a swallow. The bird was instantly killed, much to Mr. Peters' regret, but nevertheless he could not resist the opportunity to 'Ripley' the other golfers."

If the "Ripley" reference escapes you, you must be younger than 50. Google "Ripley's Believe It Or Not."

Special thanks to Wendy Davis of the Mille Lacs County Historical Society for research help on many of these courses.

CHAPTER 23

Great View, Tight Squeeze

"For the experts ... all they had to do was take an iron, lift the ball to the green and putt it down, but for those who are not as accurate with their short irons, there were plenty of difficulties."

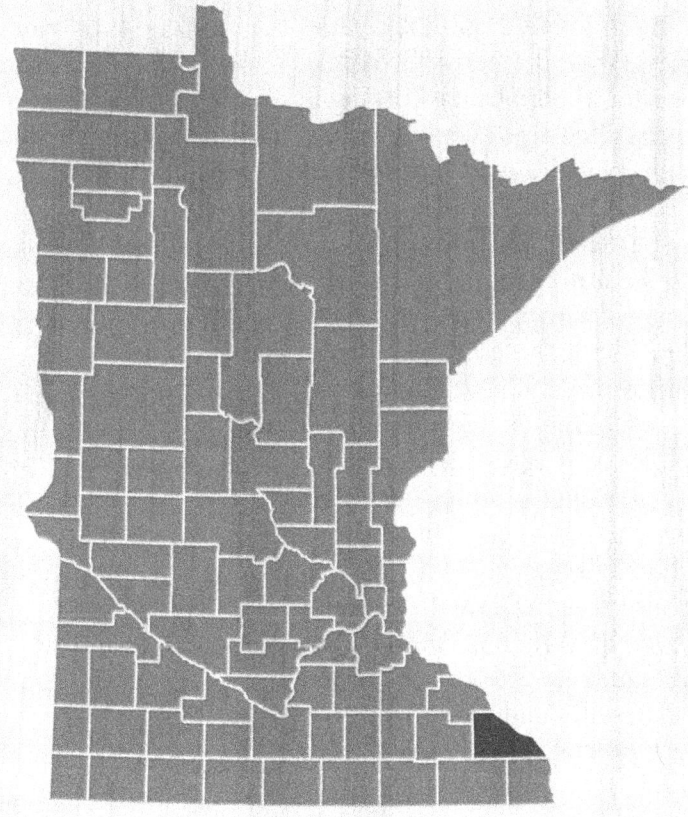

COURSE: RIVERDALE GOLF COURSE
CITY: DONEHOWER/DAKOTA
COUNTY: WINONA
YEARS: 1931–40

More! Gone.

BEN KNIGHT, THE FIRST PROFESSIONAL AT WINONA COUNTRY CLUB AND HEAD MAN THERE FOR 32 YEARS STARTING IN 1919, WAS AN AMBITIOUS AND ACCOMPLISHED FIGURE IN SOUTHEASTERN MINNESOTA GOLF. IN ADDITION TO HIS TEACHING, PLAYING AND ORGANIZING DUTIES AT WINONA CC, KNIGHT DESIGNED, BY HIS ESTIMATION IN A 1954 WINONA DAILY NEWS STORY, "ABOUT 40 OR 50" COURSES IN MINNESOTA, WISCONSIN AND IOWA.

All of which made Ben ...

... forgive me for this ...

... the Knight in shining ardor of Minnesota golf.

Spare the rim shot, and let's move on.

Operating in a hilly region known as the Driftless Area, the native Scotsman Knight became a specialist in working in tight quarters. He helped wedge a course in between hillsides and intertwined with a creek at his longtime home base on the southeast side of Winona. (Formerly Winona Country Club, the course is now known as The Bridges.) He dropped nine holes onto a Root River blufftop in 1929 at Lanesboro, southwest of Winona. He did similar work at places such as Rushford, Preston and Sleepy Eye (a geographic outlier) in Minnesota and Arcadia, Mondovi and Whitehall in Wisconsin.

Knight also designed now-lost courses in Minnesota at Winona, Wabasha and Caledonia and in Wisconsin at La Crosse, Galesville and West Salem — plus a few more, including the following lost curiosity.

———

Knight was stuck between a rock and a wet place. The former: An enormous slab of sandstone and dolomite, known as Queens Bluff, quickly rising almost 500 feet high, halfway between Winona and La Crosse on the Minnesota side. The latter: the Mississippi River. Perhaps you've heard of it.

In between: Knight's charge, likely starting in early 1931, was to build a nine-hole golf course at the bottom of the bluffside, near the unincorporated community of Donehower. This plot, shaped like a strip of bacon, offered all the architectural elbow room of a sumo wrestler in a Smart car.

On the east, Knight's boundary was Highway 3 (U.S. highways 61 and 14 in today's terms). Only 50 yards beyond that was the Mississippi River shore. On the west, Knight's boundary was the foot of the bluffs. All told, the golf course tract was an estimated 300 feet wide and 1,500 feet long — around 10 acres total.

The typical par-3 golf course, Google searches suggest, covers about 30 acres. (There are notable exceptions.)

How Knight did it is beyond me. All that comes to mind are three architectural wonders: Stonehenge, the Great Pyramid of Cheops and Ben Knight's Golf Course in a Straitjacket.

I grew up not far away and have crossed this spot at least 200 times. Until stumbling across a few newspaper stories in early 2020, I had not the foggiest idea there was ever a golf course

Great View, Tight Squeeze

TOP: The view alongside U.S. highways 14 and 61, just a few hundred yards south of the site of the old Riverdale Golf Course, likely is similar to what Riverdale golfers saw more than 80 years ago.

BOTTOM: Though this view is from just south of the Riverdale site and partway up the bluffside, it shows the severe slope of the terrain that had to have kept Riverdale designer Ben Knight from going far up the bluffside.

JOE BISSEN PHOTOS

here, and I remain stunned and captivated over how Knight could have pulled it off.

Knight's creation was called Riverdale Golf Course.

Reported the *Winona Republican-Herald* of July 28, 1931: "A new private golf course known as Riverdale, the property of George C. Phillips of La Crosse, located on Highway No. 3 a quarter of a mile north of Hunthaven Hotel, will be opened tomorrow afternoon by the Rotary and Kiwanis clubs of Winona who will be the guests of Mr. Phillips.

"The course, laid out by Ben Knight, Winona Country Club professional, cost between $10,000 and $12,000. It has nine grass greens and is 1,133 yards in length, the holes ranging in distance from 76 to 226 yards.

"Although the course is owned by Mr. Phillips, Hunthaven guests will be allowed to use it.

"... The course is between the concrete highway and the bluffs, a narrow stretch of ground, but the holes have been placed so as to use the limited space to the best advantage, some of them being high up on the bluff side, making interesting pitch shots."

The story concluded with this bit of blasphemy: "The Hunthaven swimming pool will be open to those who prefer swimming to golf."

The Hunthaven Hotel, like the golf course, also nestled up against the river bluff. Opened in 1930 and owned by E.D. Hunt of La Crosse, Hunthaven was a 50-room summer getaway that overlooked one of the most scenic stretches of highway from the Twin Cities to the Iowa border. It hosted

Hunthaven Hotel postcard, postmarked 1937 and probably dating to 1930.
CURT TEICH & CO. POSTCARD.

events for both Winona and La Crosse clientele.

Riverdale Golf Course consisted of eight par-3s and a par-4 ninth hole. It was dedicated on July 29, 1931, by about 20 Kiwanians and Rotarians from Winona. "Most of the players found the course entirely new to their game," the *Winona Republican-Herald* noted the next day. "For the experts ... all they had to do was take an iron, lift the ball to the green and putt it down, but for those who are not as accurate with their short irons, there were plenty of difficulties. The fairways are practically all rough and the player who misses the green from the tee gets in trouble."

Play at Riverdale continued into the late 1930s but likely not much beyond. Julian Johnson of La Crosse had a hole in one on the 100-yard fourth hole in September 1931, and Mailen Mills, a former all-city football and basketball player at La Crosse Central High School, aced the 105-yard seventh hole in July 1938. Course-record rounds were posted by J.R. Johnson with a 27 in 1932, Trifon Harritos with a 26 in 1936 and Harry Kubiak with a 26-29—55 in 1938.

A *Daily News* story and ad from 1935 indicated that the course would open to the public, or at least to Hunthaven guests. A *La Crosse Tribune* story from 1935 reported that Philips (likely the correct spelling of his surname, as opposed to "Phillips") had improved Riverdale, though offering no specifics on golf course improvements. "The beauty of the course is improved by the tricky shots from tee to green," the story read. "Some of the tees are on high elevations, the player playing his shot down hill to the green. On other holes the player must shoot to a high elevation to reach the green."

Given that, a best guess on the routing: It was more or less out-and-back, heading north and returning south. A handful of holes likely were in a sort of staggered, parallel formation, some heading diagonally up the bluff to the green and some returning diagonally down. Another handful of holes likely ran parallel to the highway in something of a straight line.

Adjacent or near the golf course, the Philips estate featured an arboretum and animal life, as reported by the *Tribune*: a flock of sheep, guinea hens, swans, Canada geese, green peacocks ("including the gorgeous golden") and several wild ducks.

If your social inclinations lean toward the prudish side, you may skip the following paragraph.

A May 1937 *Daily News* story said the Riverdale summer resort would open "with a new vacation feature — portable cabinets for nude sun bathing, similar to those being used in Southern resorts."

A 1940 *La Crosse Tribune* ad touted Riverdale's "sporty 9-hole golf course with bent grass greens and beautiful well-kept fairways."

That was the last mention of Riverdale Golf Course that I found. Just down the road, the Hunthaven Hotel carried on, albeit in different iterations. In 1938, C.W. Whittaker of Winona had bought Hunthaven from Gene Hunt of La Crosse and renamed it Grand View Nite Club, with intentions to include dancing and a tavern on the premises (no alcohol was to be served at Hunthaven, according to one early newspaper report). In 1952, the building was purchased by the Evangelical Lutheran Church and became Lutherhaven, a bible camp. Later, it became Riverhaven, a private secondary school. The three-story building was demolished starting in December 1975 to make way for development of O.L. Kipp State Park, now Great River Bluffs State Park.

Today, if my hours of virtually exploring the land plus conversations with those who know the neighborhood plus one trip southeast have me pointed in the right direction, the Hunthaven/Grand View/Lutherhaven/Riverhaven site is lost amid tall hardwoods and undergrowth, just north of the entrance to the state park bike-in campsites. Just north of that and near the highway are a handful of homes on or with access to Falcon Road. This is likely where the golf course lay, and advancing no farther north than the north end of Falcon Road. Old aerial photos don't reveal much, but a 1940 aerial from the University of Minnesota's John Borchert Map Library shows maybe probably just enough room to squeeze in nine short holes and maybe who knows

More! Gone.

Great View, Tight Squeeze

TOP: Along a trail on the north side of Great River Bluffs State Park near Donehower, Minn. In the foreground is Queens Bluff; on the other side of the bluff was the site of Riverdale Golf Course. Shown beyond the bluff are the Mississippi River and Wisconsin.

LEFT: A sign in Great River Bluffs State Park advises visitors to be aware of rattlesnakes, which inhabit the Mississippi River bluffsides of Winona and Houston counties. Unpleasant encounters with humans are rare.

BOTTOM: Atop the bluff and among the brush rests a marker, about 4 inches in diameter and unobtrusively only a few inches above ground, not part of a park display. It was left there, dated 1895, by the Mississippi River Commission, which oversaw improvement of the river. It features the marker's latitude, longitude and elevation (1,853 feet above sea level).

JOE BISSEN PHOTOS

probably two or three variations in the landscape that might have been greens.

Tom Ezdon, a city councilor in nearby Dakota, asked around in late 2019 and said no one he talked with remembered the Riverdale golf course but that people did remember Hunthaven, "and it was quite the place."

One of the houses on Falcon Road was owned by William T. Burgess, publisher of the La Crosse Tribune. He died in 2002, but his son, Tom, of Hudson, Wis., told me that although he knew nothing of the golf course, he did remember a path or road leading from near the house all the way up the bluff and to an orchard atop the bluff. Historic aerial photos confirm that an orchard once existed on an exposed area on the south side of Queens Bluff.

Atop the bluff, spectacular views of the Mississippi River below are afforded. Near the northernmost point in the park, atop Kings Bluff, there is one such spectacular view, with Queens Bluff in the foreground, 2,000 feet to the east. If one could just ... bend ... their eyesight ... a little around Queens Bluff, it's likely they could see a small patch of land below, featuring Falcon Road home sites and Ben Knight's tight squeeze, aka the old Riverdale Golf Course.

Back in Winona

Knight's most obscure, and maybe short-lived, design might have been in his city of residence: on the campus of St. Mary's College, now St. Mary's University, on the west side of Winona.

An April 1929 story in the *Winona Daily News* mentioned an "elimination tournament" to be played at St. Mary's. "Golf has become a very popular game at the heights in the last few years and is becoming more so each year. The colege (sic) course along the creek is kept in use in the afternoons by members of the faculty as well as half the student body."

The suspicion here is that was an informal, possibly poorly developed, course. Knight's involvement came the next year, when the school announced that work had begun on a nine-hole course "adjoining Frontenac field, the college athletic field."

The course was to be known as the Frontenac field course, and the newspaper reported that Knight would be designing it. Length was to be 3,000 yards, and the hope was that it would be ready for play by summer 1931.

"St. Mary's will have within a few years a course that in natural hazards, design and beauty of setting will be unrivaled among the college courses in the country," the *Daily News* reported. A full accounting of all nine holes followed, with the first running from the edge of the athletic field to the creek (presumably Gilmore Creek) and the last, 155 yards, going from the highway (presumably U.S. 14) to the west side of St. Mary's Hall.

The *Daily News* on May 9, 1932, reported that five intramural sports would be played at St. Mary's, including golf and quoits, a cousin to horseshoes played by throwing a ring onto a spike. "Entries for the golf tournament are not yet complete," the newspaper reported, "but the daily activities on the golf course indicates a large number of contestants."

The golf course almost certainly didn't last long. It was mentioned a handful of times in the *Daily News* for having hosted intramural meets, but I found no references to it dated past May 1932, and inquiries with two St. Mary's employees produced surprise but no knowledge of the Frontenac field course.

NOTE: I can't leave this chapter without addressing Knight's design work at Winona Country Club. The number of references I've read that give Knight full or partial credit for designing the course and the number that credit the design to prolific American golf architect Tom Bendelow are roughly equal. Even the *Daily News*, in a handful of stories spanning many years, has separately credited one or the other. I also have read stories crediting Knight with the golf course design and Bendelow with the clubhouse design, though Stuart Bendelow, Tom's grandson and author of a book on Tom's work, told me he knows of no building design work by Tom Bendelow. My suspicion is that both men worked on planning and design, and the credits have just plain been inconsistent.

CHAPTER 24

Out of Bounds? Not Really.

"The groundskeeper drove a Model-T Ford they had modified so that the back wheels were stainless steel and had spikes in them that were a good foot wide, made for pulling the lawn mowers."

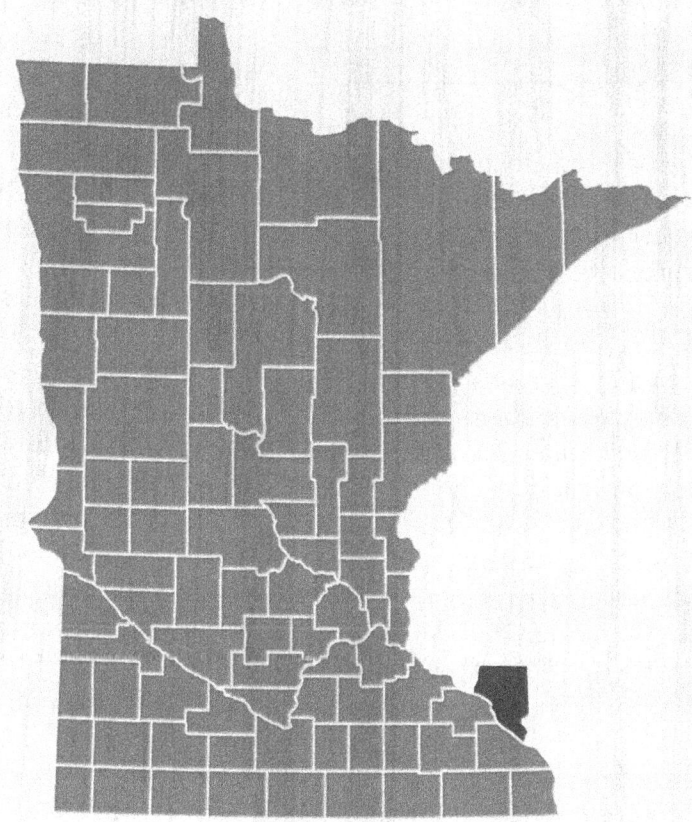

COURSE: FOUNTAIN CITY GOLF CLUB
CITY: FOUNTAIN CITY, WIS.
COUNTY: BUFFALO
YEARS: 1933–1953

More! Gone.

Like it or not, Minnesotans and Wisconsinites, and I don't see why we get burrs in our golf shoes over it, we are connected.

We cross bridges and borders to get to you. You cross bridges and borders to get to us. We eat your cheese. You eat our Spam. (Possibly at the same time, though my palate disfavors that notion.) You beat our sports teams. Once in a while, we beat yours.

With that, one last lost golf course. Yes, in Wisconsin. Why? Because connections.

John A. Latsch Jr. (1860–1934) grew up in the Wisconsin county of Trempealeau and became a successful and wealthy retail grocer in Winona, Minn. He acquired extensive land holdings in both states. The *Winona Daily* News at least once labeled him "eccentric," and whether or not that was accurate, he most certainly was philanthropic.

"In addition to the 2,200 acres of park and recreation land Latsch gave to the city of Winona," the *Daily News* reported in 2014, "he also purchased acres and acres of park land for the states of Minnesota and Wisconsin, including Trempealeau Mountain and areas of Perrot State Park and Merrick State Park."

Speaking of the latter ...

George Byron Merrick (1841–1931) was a Civil War veteran, historian, author and early Mississippi River steamboat pilot who plied the great river's waters on, one would presume, both sides of the Minnesota-Wisconsin border. He lived in Prescott, Wis.

In 1919 and 1921, Latsch donated land — variously described in reports as 266 acres or up to 5,000 acres — alongside the Mississippi River just north of Fountain City, Wis., to the state of Wisconsin. In 1932, the land became a state park, with Wisconsin honoring Latsch's request to name it for Merrick.

Hence, Merrick State Park.

Much of this area was bottomland — river back channels, islands and swamp, terrific for boating and fishing — but on a higher patch of sandy ground at the eastern edge of the park, alongside Wisconsin Highway 35, golfers got a cut of the action.

"Work has been started on the new Fountain City Bay golf course which will be open for play next year," the *Winona Daily News* reported on May 4, 1932. "The course is located on Fountain City Bay, a mile and a half north of Fountain City, on state park property."

The course would be nine holes, 3,015 yards, with sand greens, and was designed by Winona Country Club professional Ben Knight, who within three years would have laid out three courses within 15 miles of Winona: Riverdale (now defunct), the St. Mary's College course (now defunct) and Merrick State Park (you can see where this is heading).

Among his 50 or more designs, Knight also laid out the course (defunct) at Whitewater State Park near St. Charles, Minn., a park established in part on land donated by Latsch, and

Old Merrick State Park brochure, featuring a photo of the Fountain City Golf Club. "A public golf course surrounded by high stone crags and rolling hills," the brochure read, "provide(s) recreational interest for the park guest."

Westfield Golf Course in Winona, still operating, also on former Latsch land.

"The (Merrick) course is situate(d) on rolling and picturesque land," the *Daily News* continued, "part of it along the bay itself. The picnic grounds on the bay and the swimming, with which it provides, are expected to make this one of the attractive outing spots of Western Wisconsin in the summer of 1933."

Edward Kirchner of Fountain City was head of the golf club association, which had members from Fountain City, Cochrane and Alma.

Fountain City Golf Club also drew players from Winona, nine miles to the southeast as the crow flies — or as the distressed aircraft flies. Word is, Max Conrad, a famed Winona aviator for whom the city's airport is named, encountered trouble one day while airborne and had to make an emergency landing on the golf course — annoying a prominent Fountain Citian mid-round.

Adrian Morchinek, who lives just off the south edge of the state park and old golf grounds, said he remembered a fellow named Chester Wunderlich — a shorter man who needed lifts for his shoes to reach the gas pedal of his automobiles — flying a Piper Cub that he would land on the golf course grounds. Then he would disembark and play nine.

Ed Hentges of Fountain City remembered caddying for a "loner" who drove a white Packard.

"I was probably about 14," Hentges said, "and not all that perceptive. I do remember that the guy I caddied for was a very marginal golfer. It was about the time I found out I needed glasses — I was standing on the shoreline, a towboat went by and my mom said, 'You can't read the name on the towboat?' I said, 'No, I can't see it.' ... You can about imagine how far I could see the golf ball, so luckily he didn't hit it very far."

Hentges said 15 cents was the going rate for caddying nine holes.

"The groundskeeper drove a Model-T Ford they had modified so that the back wheels were stainless steel and had spikes in them that were a good foot wide, made for pulling the lawn mowers."

Sharon Hoch lives not far north of Merrick State Park. Her father, who worked for the state of Wisconsin, and mother were caretakers of the golf course. She remembered a big fireplace built next to the clubhouse, parallel to the highway, where steaks would be grilled for men's nights. Her mother would make fried potatoes in a big, black, round frying pan for the men. On ladies nights, the women would bring salads and Hoch's mother would make desserts.

"Two of the golfers that came there in men's leagues," Hoch said, "were Dr. Sheridan, he was a dentist, and Dr. Skemp. ...

"Dr. Skemp, who was a medical doctor, always golfed, and if he would get a call (in an emergency), his wife would call my mother, and then my mother would go and honk her horn on her car three times, and then she would

COURTESY OF FOUNTAIN CITY HISTORICAL MUSEUM

Out of Bounds? Not Really.

Merrick State Park, 2019. This spot, alongside a Mississippi River back channel, is not far from the southern edge of the former Fountain City Golf Club grounds.

JOE BISSEN PHOTO

wait a little bit and she would blow it three more times so they could hear it from out on the golf course so then (Dr. Skemp) would come in and she would tell him where he needed to go."

The Hochs were caretakers up until Fountain City Golf club closed, with the state intervening. "The Wisconsin Conservation Department made it clear here Wednesday afternoon it is not in the golf course business," the *Winona Daily News* reported on Oct. 1, 1953, after a public hearing in Fountain City.

C.L. Harrington, acting state forester and superintendent of state parks, and local golfer J.A. Kirchner were among those engaging in a spirited debate over the course's fate, with the state maintaining it had put money into the course without seeing suitable return and golfers saying the course couldn't be popular and viable without what they saw as proper funding from the state.

Guess who won out. It was a fait accompli, and Fountain City Golf Club at Merrick State Park soon shut down for good, presumably after the 1953 season.

The park remains in operation, offering, among other attractions, camping, hiking, a playground and two boat landings. It entertains visitors from many places, including Wisconsin, land of cheese, and Minnesota, land of Spam.

LOST GOLF COURSES: THE LIST

Minnesota's lost golf courses, 1897 through April 2020. Includes all courses known to the author, with city and confirmed or approximate years of opening and closing. This is not intended to be an all-inclusive list, but it's all that I know of.

Specific locations of almost all of the courses can be seen on a Google map I produced. View it by googling "lost golf course map."

Corrections, additions or revisions are welcome; please leave a note through ForeGoneGolf.com.

DESIGNATIONS:
M-covered in *More! Gone.*; FG-covered in *Fore! Gone.*;
W-covered on Fore.Gone.com.

Aitkin County
McGregor: Oakes / Kare Phree Pines, early to mid-1900s

Anoka
Andover: Woodland Creek Golf Club, 1989–circa 2010

Blaine: KateHaven Golf Course, 1981–2014

Columbia Heights: Hilltop Public Golf Links, 1927–46 (FG)

Coon Rapids: Jake's / Mississippi Golf Course, 1931–36 (FG)

Mounds View: The Bridges of Mounds View, 1995–2006

Becker
Detroit Lakes: Ironman Golf Course, 1960–2017

Hilltop Public Golf Links, Columbia Heights

Beltrami
Bemidji: Bemidji Municipal, 1920s–early 1940s (FG)

Benton
Foley: Foley Golf Club, 1930–36 (FG, W)

Sauk Rapids: Benton County Golf course, 1930–31 (M, W)

Lost Golf Courses: The List

Big Stone

Browns Valley: Lakeside Golf Club, Browns Valley/Beardsley, 1924–1930s (FG)

Ortonville: Ortonville Golf Club, 1922–39 (FG)

Blue Earth

Faribault: Tatepaha Golf Club / Faribault Golf & Country Club, 1900–55 (FG)

Faribault: Shattuck Golf Course, 1928–95 (FG)

Lake Crystal: Lakato Golf Club, 1923–circa 1940 (W)

Mankato: Memorial Golf Course, 1942–43 (FG)

Mankato: Southview / Ironwood Country Club, 1961–84 (FG)

Brown

Sleepy Eye: Riverside Golf Club, 1927–unknown

Carlton

Holyoke: Wilderness Hills Golf Course, 1995–unknown

Carver

Chanhassen: Mudcura Golf Club, 1926–1940s (FG)

Cass

Backus: Black Bear Golf Complex, 1998–2017

Backus: Black Bear Golf Course, 1998–unknown

Cass Lake: Cass Lake Golf Club, 1926–38 (M, W)

Fairview Township: Birch Bay Golf Course, 1965–2015

Longville: Ridgewood Golf Course, 1987–2016

Longville: Wilderness Trail Golf & Village (formerly Chippewa National), 1987–2016

Walker: Wedgewood Golf Course, 1967–2004

Chippewa

Milan: Milan Golf Club, 1922–40 (W)

Chisago

Chisago City: Chisago Golf Club, 1920–circa 1943 (FG)

Lindstrom: Chisago Lakes Par 3, 1963–65 (FG)

Rush City: Rush City Country Club, 1932–circa 1954 (M, W)

Shafer: Countryside Golf Course, 2001–circa 2012

Wyoming: Greenwood Golf Links, 1985–circa 2006

More! Gone.

Clay

Glyndon: Ponderosa Golf Club, 1964–2015

Moorhead: Town & Country Golf Course, 1963–2007

Clearwater

Clearbrook: Unknown name, circa 1930s

Gonvick: Lost River Golf Course, circa 1958–circa 2000 (W)

Cottonwood

Windom: Windom Golf Club I (north), 1922–25

Windom Golf Club II (east), 1926–1940s (FG)

Crow Wing

Brainerd: Brainerd Country Club / Pine Meadows Golf Course, 1921–2004

Fifty Lakes: Fairways at Howard's Barn, 1968–circa 2015

Nisswa: Fritz's Resort Golf Course, 1974–2006

Pine River: Irish Hills Golf Course, 1985–2009

Pine River: Pine River Country Club, 1981–2010

Dakota

Burnsville: Orchard Gardens Golf Course, 1967–2004

Eagan: Carriage Hills Golf Course, 1967–2005

Eagan: Parkview Golf Club, 1969–2013

Hastings: Hastings golf course (Conzemius site), 1924–28 (M)

Hastings: Valley View Golf Course (10th and Bailey), 1929–60 (M, W)

Lost Golf Courses: The List

Lakeville: Antlers Park Golf Links, 1926–38 (FG)

Mendota Heights: Bunker Hills Country Club, 1933–42 (FG)

Mendota Heights: Fischer's Par 3 Course, circa 1950s

Rosemount: Brockway Golf Course, 1935–2004

West St. Paul: Thompson Oaks Golf Course, 1997–2017

Thompson Oaks, West St. Paul

Douglas

Alexandria: Crestwood Golf Course, 1972–1997

Fillmore

Mabel: Meadowbrook Golf & Country Club, 1984–circa 2008

Spring Valley: Spring Valley golf course, 1929–circa 1942 (FG)

Spring Valley: Root River Country Club, 1962–2014

Freeborn

Albert Lea: Albert Lea Country Club, 1912–2006 (M, W)

Albert Lea: Albert Lea Golf Club, 1904–circa 1905 (W)

Albert Lea: Recreation Course, 1930–circa 1942 (W)

Hayward: Holiday Park Golf Course, 1966–2011

Goodhue

Wanamingo: Cannon Glen GC, 1926–unknown

Grant

Hoffman: Red Rock Golf Course, 1932–2016

Hennepin

Brooklyn Park: Joyner's (Brooklyn Park Golf Course), 1962–96 (FG)

Brooklyn Park: Scot-Tees, 1970s

Dayton: French Lake Open Golf, 1985–2015

Dayton: Hayden Hills Golf Course, 1972–2018

Deephaven: The Minnetonka Club / Burton Private Course, 1900–circa 1930 (FG)

Deephaven: St. Louis Hotel course, 1902 (M)

Eden Prairie: Cedar Hills Golf Course, 1940–2000

Edina: Fred Richards Golf Course, 1956–2014

Minneapolis: Bryn Mawr Golf Club, 1898–1910 (FG)

Minneapolis: Camden Park Golf Club, 1899–circa 1907 (M, W)

Minnetonka: Meadowwoods Golf Course, 1991–circa 2004

Minnetrista: Red Oak Golf Course, 1969–2013

Mound: Mound Golf Course, 1929–1940s (FG)

Orono: Lakeview Golf Course, 1956–2013

Plymouth: Begin Oaks Golf Course, 2000–14

Plymouth: Elm Creek Golf Course, 1960–2013

Plymouth: Felder's Golf Center, 1958–87 (FG)

Plymouth: Hampton Hills Golf Course, 1960–2003

Plymouth: Hollydale Golf Course, 1965–2019

Prior Lake: Lone Pine Golf Course, 1967–2002

Richfield: Rich Acres Golf Course, 1980–99 (FG)

St. Louis Park: Westwood Hills Golf Course, 1929–61 (FG)

Shorewood: Minnetonka Country Club, 1916–2014 (M)

Houston

Caledonia: Caledonia Golf Club I (Beranek farm), circa 1920s

Caledonia: Caledonia Golf Club II (Bowers farm), 1929–circa 1940 (FG)

Caledonia: Caledonia Golf Club III (Koenig farm), 1949 (FG)

Spring Grove: Spring Grove golf course, circa 1930s (FG)

Isanti

Cambridge: Deer Meadows Golf Course, 2000–unknown

Cambridge: Shady Oaks golf course, 1920s–circa 1950 (W)

Isanti: Bar L Ranch Club, late 1950s–1970 (W)

Itasca

Chippewa National Forest: Nopeming Private Course, 1925–72 (FG)

Grand Rapids: Wendigo Golf Club, 1995–2011

Itasca State Park: Douglas Lodge golf course, circa 1920s-1940s

Marcell: Arcadia Lodge golf course, 1926–circa 1950

Jackson

Heron Lake: Heron Lake Golf Club, 1925–1930s (FG)

Jackson: Jackson Golf Club, 1923–44 (FG)

Lakefield Golf Club, 1926–1930s (FG)

Kandiyohi

Spicer: Green Lake Country Club, 1917–circa 1945 (FG)

Kittson

Hallock: Hallock Golf Club, circa 1929–unknown (W)

Lac qui Parle

Boyd: Boyd Country Club, 1924–unknown

LOST GOLF COURSES: THE LIST

Clarkfield: Orwoll Golf Club, 1928–unknown

Le Sueur

Waterville: Shor-Tee Golf Course, 1966–94 (W)

Lincoln

Ivanhoe: Midway Golf Links, 1933–41 (W)

Lake Benton: Ben-Ti, 1924–39 (W)

Lyon

Cottonwood: Cottonwood Golf Club, 1928–unknown (W)

Marshall: Marshall Golf Club I, 1901 (M, W)

Marshall: Marshall Golf Club II, 1924–42 (M, W)

Minneota: Minneota Golf Club, 1931–unknown (W)

Russell: Russell Golf Club, 1931–unknown (W)

Tracy: Tracy Golf Club, 1921–circa 1936 (FG)

Marshall

Warren: Oakwood Golf Course, 1932–unknown (W)

Martin

Fairmont: Rolling Greens Fairways, 1977–2003

Bay View Hotel golf course, Onamia

McLeod

Brownton: Sommerdorf Golf Course, 1928–35 (FG)

Hutchinson: Hutchinson Golf Club I, 1923–25 (W)

Hutchinson: Hutchinson Golf Club II, 1927–38 (W)

Hutchinson: Meadow Links, 1999–circa 2015

Mille Lacs

Foreston: Mille Lacs County Golf Club, 1929–31 (M, W)

Milaca: Milaca Golf Club, 1932–circa 1943 (M, W)

Onamia: Bay View Hotel golf course, 1927–circa 1940s (W)

Princeton: Princeton Golf Club I (Fairgrounds), 1928–29 (M, W)

Princeton: Princeton Golf Club II (Rum River), 1929–circa 1937 (M, W)

Wahkon: Higbee's Golf Course, closed 2013

Morrison
Hillman: Sullivan Lake course, dates unknown

Mower
Austin: Hillcrest Golf Course, 1934–circa 1943 (FG)

Austin: Austin Municipal, 1931–32 (FG)

Murray
Chandler: Chandler golf course, 1920s (FG)

Fulda: Fulda golf course, 1920s

Slayton: Tri City Golf Club / Murray Golf Club / Slayton Golf and Country Club, 1926–49 (W)

Nicollet
Fairfax: Fort Ridgely State Park Golf Course, 1927–2017

Nobles
Worthington: Prairie View Golf Links, 1983–2015

Norman
Ada Golf Club I, Ada, 1900–unknown (M, W)

Ada Golf Club II, Ada, 1930–circa 1937 (M, W)

Twin Valley: Twin Valley Golf Course, 1926–1930s (M)

Olmsted
Byron: Links of Byron, 1994–circa 2013

Elgin: Elgin Golf Club, 1931–32 (W)

Rochester: Meadow Lakes Golf Course, 1998–2012

Rochester: Silver Creek Golf Course, 1900–unknown (M, W)

Stewartville: Maplebrook Golf Course, 1974–unknown

Otter Tail
Dent: Rock Pile Golf Course, 1999–2013

Fergus Falls: Fergus Golf Club, 1901 (W)

Fergus Falls: Riverside Links, 1922–40 (W)

Pelican Rapids: Rolling Hills Golf Course, circa 1970–2016

Pine
Hinckley: Hinckley Golf Club, 1929–36 (M)

Pine City: Pine City Golf Links (Fairgrounds), 1925–30 (M)

Pokegama Township: McAllen Golf Course, 1931–circa 1936 (M)

Pipestone
Pipestone: Pipestone Golf Club I (Even farm); golf in Pipestone dates to 1923 or earlier

Pipestone: Pipestone Golf Club II (Hines farm): dates unknown

Pipestone: Pipestone Golf Club III (Indian Lakes)

Polk
Fertile: Fertile Golf Club, 1928–unknown (W)

Lost Golf Courses: The List

Ramsey

Gem Lake: Matoska Golf Club, 1923–38 (FG)

Maplewood: Country View Golf Course, 1930–2004

Maplewood: Maple Hills Golf Course, 1954–2003

North St. Paul: Northwood Country Club, 1915–45 (FG)

St. Paul: The Lake Park Golf Club, 1922 (M, W)

St. Paul: Lakeview / Hillcrest Golf Club, 1921–2017 (M, W)

Lakeview/Hillcrest Golf Club, St. Paul
VALERIE REICHEL PHOTOS

St. Paul: Merriam Park Golf Club, 1900-06 (FG)

St. Paul: Quality Park, 1925–unknown (FG)

St. Paul: Roadside Golf Club, 1897–1903 (FG)

Red Lake

Red Lake Falls: Red Lake Falls Golf Club (Demarais Farm), 1930–32 (M, W)

Oklee: Oklee Golf Course, circa 1963–circa 1976 (W)

Renville

Renville Golf Club (Fairgrounds), 1928 (W)

Rice

Northfield: Northfield Golf Club, mid-1920s-1926

Rock

Beaver Creek: Beaver Creek Golf Course, 2003–07

Luverne: Luverne Golf Club (Gabrielson farm), 1925–32 (M, W)

Luverne: Luverne Golf Club (Rock River site), 1933–38 (M, W)

Roseau

Roseau: Roseau golf course (Fairgrounds), moved in 1936

Warroad: Warroad Golf Clubs I and II (Bloom School and the Estates), references found in 1936 and 1941

Scott

Belle Plaine: Valley View Golf Club, 1992–2015

Sherburne

Elk River: Elk River Golf Club, 1924–42 (W)

St. Cloud: Teachers College course, 1931-mid-1930s (M, W)

St. Louis

Britt: Sand Lake golf course, 1914–unknown

Chisholm: Chisholm Public Golf Course, 1927–circa 1941 (FG)

Duluth: Lakewood Golf Club, 1931–1941 (FG)

Duluth: Riverside Golf Club, 1919–44 (FG)

Duluth: Unknown name, circa 1900

Hermantown: Maple Grove Golf Acres, 1972–81, 1984 (FG)

Mountain Iron: Midiron Country Club, 1927–circa 1940

Tower: Everett Point Golf Course, 1921–circa 1940s (FG)

Stearns

Cold Spring: City View Golf Course, 1999–2015 (M, W)

Cold Spring: Scenic Golf Course (Cold Spring Golf Club), 1930s (M, W)

Collegeville: St. John's course, circa 1926–33 (FG)

Richmond: Chain O' Lakes Golf Course, 1931–circa 1941 (M, W)

St. Augusta: Springbrook Golf Course, 1930-mid-1930s (M, W)

Lost Golf Courses: The List

St. Cloud: Hillside Golf Course, 1930–45 (FG)

St. Cloud: St. Cloud Golf Club, 1899–circa 1905 (M, W)

St. Joseph: Wildwood golf course, 1929–circa-mid-1930s (M, W)

Steele

Blooming Prairie: Blooming Prairie GC, circa 1030s-1950s

Owatonna: Hidden Creek Golf Club, 1996–2009

Swift

Kerkhoven: Kerkhoven Golf Course (southeast), 1931–unknown (W)

Kerkhoven: Kerkhoven golf course (northeast), 1975–unknown

Wabasha

Lake City: Lake City Golf Club (original), 1923–29 (W)

Lake City Golf Club, Lake City

Wabasha: Wabasha Golf Club, 1927–circa 1942 (FG)

Wadena

Menahga: Menahga golf course, dates unknown

Washington

Bayport: Bayport Golf Club, 1922–35 (FG)

Bayport: Stillwater Prison course, mid-1970s (FG)

Cottage Grove: All Seasons Golf, 1993–circa 2006

Cottage Grove: Mississippi Dunes Golf Course, 1995–2017

Lake Elmo: Country Air Golf, circa 2010s

Lake Elmo: Mulligan Masters, 2004–2007

Lake Elmo: Tartan Park, 1965–2015

Oakdale: Castle Greens, 1960–82 (M)

Oakdale: Oakdale Greens / Oakdale Par 3, 1983–2009

Sauk Centre: Sauk Centre Country Club, 1921–2013

Scandia: Eko Backen golf course, 1970s (FG)

Woodbury: Woodbury Par 3, 1975–2003

Watonwan

Madelia: Madelia Golf Club, 1921–circa 1930 (M, W)

Winona

Donehower / Dakota: Riverdale Golf Course, 1931–40 (M)

Elba Township: Whitewater Valley Golf Course, 1928–75 (FG)

Winona: Winona Golf Club, 1897 (FG)

More! Gone.

Oakdale Greens/Oakdale Par 3, Oakdale (2019 photo by Joe Bissen)

Winona: Meadow-Brook Golf Club, 1898–1918 (FG)

Winona: St. Mary's College campus course, 1931–32 (M)

Wright

Annandale: Clearwater Country Club, 1925–circa 1927 (W)

Clearwater: Driftwood Golf & Fitness, 1994–2019

Howard Lake: The Greens of Howard Lake, 1995–2013

Monticello: Silver Springs Golf Course, 1974–2009

Otsego: Stone Bridge Golf Course, 1999–2009

Bucket List

Are there any lost courses in Minnesota you wish you could have played? How about any current Minnesota courses you'd like to play but haven't?

_____
_____
_____
_____
_____
_____
_____
_____
_____
_____
_____
_____
_____
_____

Be sure to visit ForeGoneGolf.com to post your favorites!

"It took me 17 years to get
3,000 hits in baseball.
I did it in one afternoon
on the golf course."

HANK AARON

www.ingramcontent.com/pod-product-compliance
Lightning Source LLC
Chambersburg PA
CBHW060423010526

44118CB00017B/2334